Grammar clear

KB132573

중학 영문법
클리어.

Level 3

문법 개념과 내신을 한번에 끝내는
중학 영문법 클리어

| 문장 구조 시각화로 **핵심 문법 개념 CLEAR!**
| 시험포인트 및 비교포인트로 **헷갈리는 문법 CLEAR!**
| 더 확대된 실전테스트로 **학교 시험 대비 CLEAR!**

학습자의 마음을 읽는 동아영어콘텐츠연구팀
동아영어콘텐츠연구팀은 동아출판의 영어 개발 연구원, 현장 선생님, 그리고 전문 원고 집필자들이
공동연구를 통해 최적의 콘텐츠를 개발하는 연구조직입니다.

원고 개발에 참여하신 분들
강남숙 신영주 이유진 최현진 홍미정 홍석현

교재 검토에 도움을 주신 분들
강군필 강은주 고미선 김민성 김은영 김우경 김호성 백명숙 신영주 이상훈
이지혜 임남주 정나래 정은주 정혜승 조수진 조은혜 최재천 최현진 한지영

중학 영문법

클리어.

Level 3

STRUCTURES 구성과 특징

1 | 문장 시각화로 핵심 문법을 한 눈에 이해!

unit 2 목적격보어의 형태 1

1 목적격보어로 명사를 쓰는 경우

동사가 call, name, elect, make, choose 등일 때

| She | named | him | Dan. | (him = Dan) |
| | made | | a superstar. | (him = a superstar) |

2 목적격보어로 형용사를 쓰는 경우

동사가 make, think, keep, find, consider, believe, leave 등일 때

| I | made | my sister | happy. | 내 여동생을 행복하게 |
| | left | | alone. | 내 여동생을 외롭게 |

목적격보어로 쓰인 형용사는 우리말로 '~하게'라고 해석되는데, 이 때문에 부사를 쓰지 않도록 주의한다.

3 목적격보어로 to부정사를 쓰는 경우

동사가 want, allow, ask, get, order, tell, advise, expect 등일 때

| Mom | wanted | me | to save more money. | 내가 돈을 더 모으기를 |
| | allowed | | to go to the concert. | 내가 콘서트에 가는 것을 |

get은 '~하게 하다'라는 의미로 쓰일 경우, 목적격보어로 to부정사를 쓴다.
He got them to set up the tent.

4 목적격보어로 동사원형 또는 현재분사를 쓰는 경우

see, watch, hear, feel, notice 등의 지각동사는 목적격보어로 동사원형이나 현재분사를 쓸 수 있다.
현재분사를 쓰면 그 시점에 동작이 진행 중임을 나타낸다.

| Kevin | saw | the children | play[playing] in the yard. | 아이들이 노는 것을 |
| | heard | | sing[singing] in the park. | 아이들이 노래하는 것을 |

2 비교 point make의 쓰임 구분

Alice made me salad. <me ≠ salad> Alice는 나에게 샐러드를 만들어 주었다. <4형식>

Alice made me a movie star. <me = a movie star> Alice는 나를 영화배우로 만들었다. <5형식>

014 중학영문법 솔리어 LEVEL 3

---

3 개념 우선 확인 | 옳은 표현 고르기

1 나를 슬프게 만들다	2 나를 'Baby'라고 부르다	3 땅이 흔들리는 것을 느끼다
☐ make me sad	☐ call Baby me	☐ feel the earth to shake
☐ make me sadly	☐ call me Baby	☐ feel the earth shaking

A 괄호 안에서 알맞은 것을 고르시오.

1 Ms. Ford told the kids (play / to play) outside.
2 Many people found the book very (interesting / interestingly).
3 I felt someone (touching / touched) my arm.
4 Sam asked me (sending / to send) him a text message.
5 They elected Joe (their leader / to their leader).

B 우리말과 일치하도록 괄호 안의 말을 이용하여 문장을 완성하시오.

1 나는 어젯밤에 한 남자가 그 집에 들어가는 것을 보았다. (enter)
→ I saw a man _____ the house last night.
2 의사는 아버지에게 규칙적으로 운동을 하라고 조언했다. (exercise)
→ The doctor advised my father _____ regularly.
3 학생들은 Timmy가 반장이 되기를 바란다. (become)
→ The students want Timmy _____ class president.

C 밑줄 친 부분을 어법에 맞게 고쳐 쓰시오.

1 Did you hear a dog to bark last night?
2 My father didn't allow me use his laptop.
3 These boots will keep your feet warmly.
4 Judy will get her brother carry her suitcase.
5 I don't want to call a liar to him.

4 30초 완성 map

목적격보어의 형태	명사	We chose Jimmy our leader.	우리는 Jimmy를 _____ 선택했다.
	형용사	I made Jimmy happy.	나는 Jimmy를 _____ 만들었다.
	to부정사	I allowed Jimmy to go there.	나는 Jimmy가 그곳에 _____ 허락했다.
	동사원형/현재분사	I heard Jimmy sing[singing].	나는 Jimmy가 _____ 들었다.

Chapter 01 문장의 구조 015

---

❶ 핵심 문법 개념 확인

문장 구조를 시각화하여 꼭 알아야 할 핵심 기본 문법들을 이해하기 쉽게 설명

❸ 개념 우선 확인

본격적인 문제로 넘어가기 전 문법 개념 이해를 다시 한번 확인하는 단계

❷ 시험 POINT & 비교 POINT

시험에 자주 나오거나 혼동되는 문법 개념들을 다시 한번 짚어주고 복습하는 장치

❹ 30초 완성 MAP

다음 Unit으로 넘어가기 전에 map을 완성하며 해당 Unit의 문법 개념을 잘 이해했는지 확인하는 코너

2 | 서술형 집중 훈련 & 시험 출제 포인트 확인

서술형 대비 문장 쓰기

- 서술형 쓰기에 많이 나오는 4가지 유형(문장 완성, 오류 수정, 문장 전환, 영작 완성)을 집중 훈련

시험에 꼭 나오는 출제 포인트

- 시험에 꼭 나오는 중요한 문법 출제 포인트를 한번 더 확인
- 고득점 Point로 내신 고난도 문제 대비

3 | 실전 TEST로 학교 시험 완벽 대비

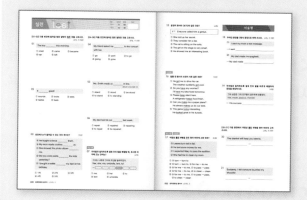

실전 TEST

- 어려워진 내신 시험에 대비하기 위한 최신 기출 유형과 고난도 유형 반영
- 서술형 문항 추가로 학교 시험 완벽 대비

+ WORKBOOK

본책 학습 뒤 Unit마다 2쪽으로 구성된 연습문제를 풀며 부족한 부분을 추가로 학습할 수 있도록 구성

- 개념 확인, 어법 선택, 어법 수정, 문장 전환, 영작 등 학습 유형별 문제 제시로 자학자습 효과 향상

 CONTENTS 차례

품사란 단어의 역할이나 쓰임새를 말한다. 영어에는 명사, 대명사, 동사, 형용사, 부사, 전치사, 접속사, 감탄사의 8품사가 있다.

명사 Noun

사람이나 사물, 장소 등의 이름을 나타내는 말이다. 명사는 문장에서 주어, 목적어, 보어로 쓰인다.

예 book, dog, girl, student, Mike, Korea, friendship, peace, love 등

Kate is very honest. 주어
My friends like **soccer** very much. 목적어
The girl is a **student**. 보어

대명사 Pronoun

명사를 대신하는 말이다. 명사처럼 문장에서 주어, 목적어, 보어로 쓰인다.

예 I, you, she, him, us, theirs, it, myself, this, that 등

You are my best friend. 주어
I bought **it** at the market. 목적어
This cell phone is **hers**. 보어

동사 Verb

사람이나 사물의 동작이나 상태를 나타내는 말이다. 동사에는 be동사와 일반동사, 조동사가 있다.

예 be, come, have, sing, visit, can, will, must, may, should 등

They **are** at the amusement park. be동사
He **played** the piano for me. 일반동사
You **must** keep the traffic rules. 조동사

형용사 Adjective

사람이나 사물의 상태나 색깔, 모양, 크기, 성질 등을 나타내는 말이다. 형용사는 문장에서 명사나 대명사를 꾸미는 수식어로 쓰이거나 주어나 목적어를 보충 설명해 주는 보어로 쓰인다.

예 pretty, handsome, tall, hungry, smart, big, long 등

I saw a **tall** tower in the city. 명사 수식
The doll is very **cute**. 주격보어
He made me **happy**. 목적격보어

부사 Adverb

시간, 장소, 방법, 정도, 빈도 등을 나타내는 말이다. 부사는 문장에서 동사나 형용사, 다른 부사, 문장 전체를 꾸며준다.

예 fast, hard, carefully, always, very, today, yesterday 등

He walked **slowly**. 동사 수식
We were **really** tired. 형용사 수식
I can speak English **very** well. 부사 수식

전치사 Preposition

명사나 대명사 앞에 쓰여 시간, 장소, 방향, 이유, 수단 등의 뜻을 더해주는 말이다.

예 at, on, in, under, from, by, with, for, during 등

I met my friends **at** two o'clock. 시간
My family lived **in** San Francisco. 장소
They went to Busan **by** train. 수단

접속사 Conjunction

단어와 단어, 구와 구, 절과 절을 연결해주는 말이다.

예 and, but, or, that, because, if 등

He studied very hard, **but** he failed the test.
We know **that** he is honest.
I was late for school **because** I got up late.

감탄사 Interjection

말하는 사람의 기쁨, 슬픔, 놀람 등의 감정을 나타내는 말이다.

예 oh, wow, oops, hooray 등

Wow, it's amazing!
Oh, she is beautiful!

* 한 단어가 하나의 품사로만 쓰이는 것은 아니다. 여러 품사로 쓰일 수 있는 단어가 있으므로 문장에서의 쓰임을 통해 품사를 파악해야 한다.

Quiz ❶ 밑줄 친 단어의 품사를 쓰시오.

	Mia	looks	sleepy	because	she	got up	early	in	the morning.
품사							부사	전치사	

2 | 문장의 구성 요소

문장을 이루는 구성 요소에는 **주어**, **동사**, **목적어**, **보어**, **수식어**가 있다.

주어 Subject

동작이나 상태의 주체가 되는 말로, '~은/는/이/가'로 해석한다. 주어는 보통 문장 맨 앞에 오고 그 뒤에 동사가 온다.

He is a popular K-pop star. **그는** 인기 있는 K-pop 팝 스타이다.

Mina visited her grandparents every month. **미나는** 매달 그녀의 조부모님을 방문했다.

동사 Verb

주어의 동작이나 상태를 나타내는 말로, '~이다/하다'로 해석한다. 동사는 주로 주어 뒤에 온다.

We **play** soccer every morning. 우리는 매일 아침 축구를 **한다**. 〈동작〉

They **are** happy. 그들은 행복**하다**. 〈상태〉

목적어 Object

동사의 대상이 되는 말로, '~을/를' 또는 '~에게'로 해석한다. 목적어는 주로 동사 뒤에 온다.

He bought **a guitar** for me. 그는 나를 위해 **기타를** 샀다.

Mom made **me gloves**. 엄마는 **나에게 장갑을** 만들어 주셨다.

보어 Complement

주어나 목적어를 보충 설명해 주는 말이다. 주격보어는 주로 동사 뒤에 오고, 목적격보어는 목적어 뒤에 온다.

He is **my father**. 그는 **나의 아버지**이다. 〈주격보어: 주어 He를 보충 설명〉

The news made me **sad**. 그 소식은 나를 **슬프게** 했다. 〈목적격보어: 목적어 me를 보충 설명〉

수식어 Modifier

다른 구성 요소를 꾸며 의미를 더해 주는 말이다.

She **usually** has breakfast **at 8**. 그녀는 **보통 8시에** 아침을 먹는다.

Quiz ❷ **밑줄 친 말의 문장 구성 요소를 쓰시오.**

	Ben	is	my dog.	I	love	him	very much.
구성 요소							

개념 우선 확인 | 밑줄 친 부분의 역할 고르기

1 She became a <u>scientist</u>.
□ 주격보어
□ 목적어

2 They bought me <u>cookies</u>.
□ 간접목적어
□ 직접목적어

3 She made me <u>happy</u>.
□ 목적어
□ 목적격보어

A 괄호 안에서 알맞은 것을 고르시오.

1 She (looked / smiled) happily with her family.

2 They like (tell / telling) stories about their lives.

3 My father (calls / tells) me Little Prince.

4 I want you (play / to play) the song for everyone.

5 My aunt bought (me / for me) this doll.

B 밑줄 친 부분을 어법에 맞게 고쳐 쓰시오.

1 They kept <u>quietly</u> during the ceremony.

2 Sue gave a birthday gift <u>for</u> her sister.

3 Joe made this sandwich <u>me</u>.

4 She said nothing to him. This made him <u>angrily</u>.

C 우리말과 일치하도록 괄호 안의 말을 바르게 배열하여 문장을 완성하시오.

1 Eric은 우리에게 근사한 식사를 요리해 주었다. (us, cooked, nice, a, meal)
  → Eric _____.

2 내 이름은 민호이지만 내 친구들은 나를 '민'이라고 부른다. (my, Min, call, friends, me)
  → My name is Minho, but _____.

3 나는 이번 주말에 Daniel과 함께 공부하고 싶다. (Daniel, to, with, study)
  → I want _____ this weekend.

30초 완성 map

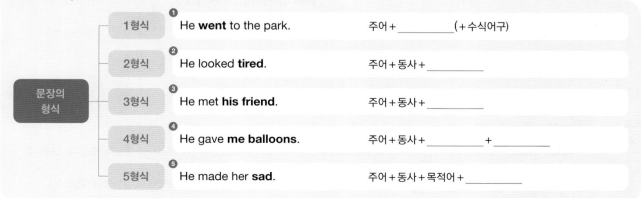

1형식	❶ He **went** to the park.	주어 + _____ (+ 수식어구)	
2형식	❷ He looked **tired**.	주어 + 동사 + _____	
3형식	❸ He met **his friend**.	주어 + 동사 + _____	
4형식	❹ He gave **me balloons**.	주어 + 동사 + _____ + _____	
5형식	❺ He made her **sad**.	주어 + 동사 + 목적어 + _____	

문장의 형식

목적격보어의 형태 1

1 목적격보어로 명사를 쓰는 경우

동사가 call, name, elect, make, choose 등일 때

| She | named | him | **Dan.** | 〈him = Dan〉 |
| | made | | **a superstar.** | 〈him = a superstar〉 |

2 목적격보어로 형용사를 쓰는 경우

동사가 make, think, keep, find, consider, believe, leave 등일 때

| I | made | my sister | **happy.** | 내 여동생을 행복하게 |
| | left | | **alone.** | 내 여동생을 외롭게 |

주의 목적격보어로 쓰인 형용사는 우리말로 '~하게'라고 해석되는데, 이 때문에 부사를 쓰지 않도록 주의한다.

3 목적격보어로 to부정사를 쓰는 경우

동사가 want, allow, ask, get, order, tell, advise, expect 등일 때

| Mom | wanted | me | **to save** more money. | 내가 돈을 더 모으기를 |
| | allowed | | **to go** to the concert. | 내가 콘서트에 가는 것을 |

▶ get은 '~가 …하게 하다'라는 의미로 쓰일 경우, 목적격보어로 to부정사를 쓴다.
He **got** them **to set up** the tent.

4 목적격보어로 동사원형 또는 현재분사를 쓰는 경우

see, watch, hear, feel, notice 등의 지각동사는 목적격보어로 동사원형이나 현재분사를 쓸 수 있다.
현재분사를 쓰면 그 시점에 동작이 진행 중임을 나타낸다.

| Kevin | saw | the children | **play** [playing] in the yard. | 아이들이 노는 것을 |
| | heard | | **sing** [singing] in the park. | 아이들이 노래하는 것을 |

비교 point

make의 쓰임 구분

Alice made me salad.　　　< me ≠ salad >　　　Alice는 나에게 샐러드를 만들어 주었다. 〈4형식〉
　　　　　간·목　적·목

Alice made me a movie star. < me = a movie star >　　Alice는 나를 영화배우로 만들었다. 〈5형식〉
　　　　　목적어　목적격보어

개념 우선 확인 | 옳은 표현 고르기

1 나를 슬프게 만들다

☐ make me sad
☐ make me sadly

2 나를 '아기'라고 부르다

☐ call Baby me
☐ call me Baby

3 땅이 흔들리는 것을 느끼다

☐ feel the earth to shake
☐ feel the earth shaking

A 괄호 안에서 알맞은 것을 고르시오.

1 Ms. Ford told the kids (play / to play) outside.

2 Many people found the book very (interesting / interestingly).

3 I felt someone (touching / touched) my arm.

4 Sam asked me (sending / to send) him a text message.

5 They elected Joe (their leader / to their leader).

B 우리말과 일치하도록 괄호 안의 말을 이용하여 문장을 완성하시오.

1 나는 어젯밤에 한 남자가 그 집에 들어가는 것을 보았다. (enter)

→ I saw a man _____ the house last night.

2 의사는 아버지에게 규칙적으로 운동을 하라고 조언했다. (exercise)

→ The doctor advised my father _____ regularly.

3 학생들은 Timmy가 반장이 되기를 바란다. (become)

→ The students want Timmy _____ class president.

C 밑줄 친 부분을 어법에 맞게 고쳐 쓰시오.

1 Did you hear a dog to bark last night?

2 My father didn't allow me use his laptop.

3 These boots will keep your feet warmly.

4 Judy will get her brother carry her suitcase.

5 I don't want to call a liar to him.

30초 완성 map

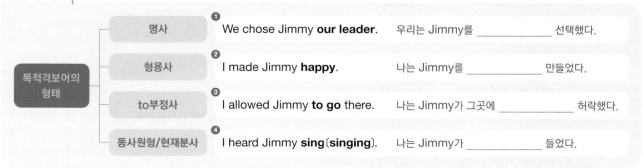

목적격보어의 형태	명사	❶ We chose Jimmy **our leader**.	우리는 Jimmy를 _____ 선택했다.
	형용사	❷ I made Jimmy **happy**.	나는 Jimmy를 _____ 만들었다.
	to부정사	❸ I allowed Jimmy **to go** there.	나는 Jimmy가 그곳에 _____ 허락했다.
	동사원형/현재분사	❹ I heard Jimmy **sing**(**singing**).	나는 Jimmy가 _____ 들었다.

1 목적격보어로 동사원형을 쓰는 경우

사역동사로 쓰인 make, have, let은 목적어와 목적격보어가 능동 관계일 때 목적격보어로 동사원형을 쓴다.
이때 사역동사는 '~가 …하게 하다'라는 의미를 나타낸다.

주어	동사	목적어	목적격보어	
The teacher	made	us	**study** hard.	우리가 열심히 공부하게
	had		**clean** the classroom.	우리가 교실을 청소하게
	let		**read** the book.	우리가 책을 읽게

└─ 능동 관계 ─┘

Sad movies always **make** me **cry**.
He **had** us **plan** the party.
I **let** my sister **wear** my new T-shirt.

▶ help가 '~가 …하는 것을 돕다'라는 의미로 쓰일 때는 목적격보어로 동사원형이나 to부정사를 쓴다.
　 She **helped** me **find** my dog.
　 = She **helped** me **to find** my dog.

2 목적격보어로 과거분사를 쓰는 경우

목적어와 목적격보어가 수동 관계일 때 과거분사를 쓴다.
동사로는 사역동사(have, make), 지각동사, find, keep, get 등이 주로 쓰인다.

주어	동사	목적어	목적격보어	
I	got	my bike	**fixed**.	내 자전거가 수리됨
She	had	her car	**checked**.	차가 점검됨
We	found	the baby	**left** alone.	아기가 혼자 남겨짐

└─ 수동 관계 ─┘

▶ 목적어와 목적격보어가 능동 관계이면 동사에 따라 목적격보어로 동사원형, to부정사, 현재분사를 쓰고, 수동
　 관계이면 과거분사를 쓴다.
　 Junho heard someone <u>**call**(**calling**)</u> his name. 준호는 누군가가 그의 이름을 **부르는** 것을 들었다.
　　　　　　　└ 능동 관계 ┘
　 Junho heard <u>his name **called**</u>. 준호는 그의 이름이 **불리는** 것을 들었다.
　　　　　　　└ 수동 관계 ┘

비교
point **사역동사의 목적격보어 vs. get의 목적격보어**
목적어와 목적격보어가 능동 관계일 때 사역동사 make, have, let은 목적격보어로 동사원형을, get은 to부정사를 쓴다.
1 He had me (carry / to carry) these boxes.
2 He got me (carry / to carry) these boxes.

개념 우선 확인 | 옳은 표현 고르기

1 그들을 오게 하다
- ☐ make them come
- ☐ make them to come

2 나를 가게 하다
- ☐ let me go
- ☐ let me gone

3 내 가방을 도둑맞다
- ☐ get my bag to steal
- ☐ get my bag stolen

A 괄호 안에서 알맞은 것을 고르시오.

1 Her teacher made her (write / to write) the report again.

2 Will you help me (install / installed) this app?

3 My father has his car (wash / washed) every weekend.

4 You can keep food (freeze / frozen) longer with dry ice.

B 밑줄 친 부분을 어법에 맞게 고쳐 쓰시오.

1 They will have the wall paint this Sunday.

2 Anna never lets anyone to enter her room.

3 What made you changed your mind?

4 I heard my favorite song singing by someone.

5 Jenny was busy, but she helped us finished the project.

C 우리말과 일치하도록 괄호 안의 말을 이용하여 문장을 완성하시오.

1 그녀의 부모님은 그녀가 패스트푸드를 못 먹게 하신다. (let, eat)

→ Her parents don't _____ _____ _____ fast food.

2 엄마는 자주 내가 설거지를 하게 한다. (make, do)

→ My mom often _____ _____ _____ the dishes.

3 그는 한 달에 한 번 그의 머리카락을 자른다. (have, hair, cut)

→ He _____ _____ _____ _____ once a month.

4 그녀는 아침에 창문이 깨져있는 것을 발견했다. (find, the window, break)

→ She _____ _____ _____ _____ in the morning.

30초 완성 map

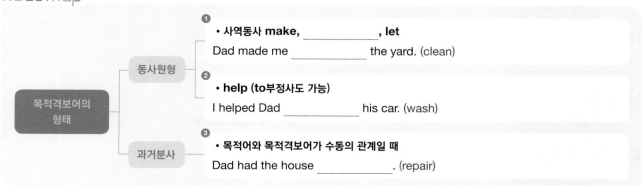

목적격보어의 형태

동사원형
- **①** 사역동사 **make,** _____ **, let**
  Dad made me _____ the yard. (clean)
- **②** **help (to부정사도 가능)**
  I helped Dad _____ his car. (wash)

과거분사
- **③** 목적어와 목적격보어가 수동의 관계일 때
  Dad had the house _____ . (repair)

Answers p. 2

≡ 배열 영작 괄호 안의 말을 바르게 배열하기

01 우리 부모님은 내가 밤에 외출하는 것을 절대 허락하지 않으신다. (allow, go out, me, to)

→ My parents never _____ at night.

02 크리스마스 무렵에는 밴드가 캐럴을 연주하는 것을 들을 수 있다. (carols, playing, hear, the band)

→ You can _____ around Christmas.

03 Emily는 내가 이 일을 빨리 끝낼 수 있게 도왔다. (helped, finish, me, this work)

→ Emily _____ early.

04 우리는 네가 우리와 같이 영화를 보러 가기를 원한다. (to, the movies, you, go, want, to)

→ We _____ with us.

✓ 오류 수정 어법에 맞게 문장 고쳐 쓰기

05 He lent some money me last week.

→ He lent _____ last week.

06 I saw a big bird to fly over my head.

→ I saw _____ over my head.

07 Jenny got me fix her computer yesterday.

→ Jenny got _____ yesterday.

08 She had her son to paint the fence.

→ She had _____ the fence.

□ 빈칸 완성 괄호 안의 말을 이용하여 빈칸 완성하기

09 엄마는 나에게 집에 오는 길에 우유를 사 오게 하셨다. (make, buy)

→ My mom _____ some milk on my way home.

10 나는 누군가가 우리 현관문을 두드리는 소리를 들었다. (hear, knock, someone)

→ I _____ on our front door.

11 그는 그의 이름이 칠판에 쓰여 있는 것을 발견했다. (find, write, his name)

→ He _____ on the blackboard.

12 우리 선생님은 우리에게 교실에서 기다리라고 말씀하셨다. (tell, wait)

→ Our teacher _____ in the classroom.

시험에 꼭 나오는 출제 포인트

출제 포인트 1 make처럼 여러 형식으로 쓰이는 동사에 주의하자!

〈보기〉의 밑줄 친 부분과 쓰임이 같은 것은?

> 보기   I <u>made</u> him open the door.

① Tom <u>made</u> this chair for Mary.
② How did you <u>make</u> this boat?
③ I <u>made</u> a birthday cake for my mom.
④ She <u>made</u> me wait for half an hour.
⑤ My grandmother <u>made</u> me a pretty doll.

출제 포인트 2 보어 자리에 형용사가 아닌 부사를 쓰지 않도록 주의하자!

빈칸에 들어갈 말로 알맞지 <u>않은</u> 것은?

> It will keep the water _____ .

① warm   ② cool   ③ hot
④ freshly   ⑤ clean

출제 포인트 3 사역동사 make, have, let은 목적격보어로 동사원형을 쓴다!

빈칸에 들어갈 말로 알맞지 <u>않은</u> 것은?

> Mr. Jackson _____ us to read some books.

① asked   ② made   ③ advised
④ told   ⑤ wanted

> **고득점 POINT** get은 '~에게 …하게 하다'라는 의미일 때 목적격보어로 to부정사를 쓴다.
>
> **우리말과 일치하도록 괄호 안의 말을 이용하여 문장을 완성하시오.**
>
> 그녀는 그에게 그의 방을 청소하게 했다. (clean)
> → She got him _____ his room.

출제 포인트 4 목적어와 목적격보어가 능동 관계인지 수동 관계인지 파악하자!

빈칸에 들어갈 말로 알맞은 것을 <u>모두</u> 고르면?

> I heard someone _____ loudly.

① shout   ② shouts   ③ shouted
④ shouting   ⑤ to shout

> **고득점 POINT** 목적격보어의 형태 파악
>
> **각 빈칸에 move를 알맞은 형태로 쓰시오.**
>
> (1) My mom had us _____ the table.
> (2) My mom had the table _____ .

유형	문항수	배점	점수
객관식	17	60	
서술형	10	40	

[01-02] 다음 빈칸에 들어갈 말로 알맞지 <u>않은</u> 것을 고르시오.
|6점, 각 3점|

01

> The boy _____ this morning.

① cried　　② came　　③ became
④ ran　　⑤ left

02

> It _____ great!

① sounds　　② looks　　③ sees
④ tastes　　⑤ feels

03 빈칸에 for가 들어갈 수 있는 것의 개수는?　　|3점|

> ⓐ He taught science _____ them.
> ⓑ My mom made cookies _____ us.
> ⓒ She showed the photo album _____ me.
> ⓓ Did you cook pasta _____ the kids yesterday?
> ⓔ I bought a wallet _____ my dad on his birthday.

① 1개　　② 2개　　③ 3개
④ 4개　　⑤ 5개

[04-06] 다음 빈칸에 들어갈 말로 알맞은 것을 고르시오.
|6점, 각 2점|

04

> My friend asked me _____ to the concert with her.

① go　　② went　　③ to go
④ going　　⑤ gone

05

> Ms. Smith made us _____ in line.
> *stand in line 줄을 서다

① stand　　② stood　　③ be stood
④ to stand　　⑤ to standing

06

> My dad had his car _____ last week.

① repair　　② repaired　　③ repairing
④ to repair　　⑤ be repaired

최신기출
07 우리말과 일치하도록 괄호 안의 말을 배열할 때, 표시된 위치에 오는 단어는?　　|4점|

> 그녀는 나에게 그녀의 우산을 빌려주었다.
> (her, she, me, umbrella, lent, to)
>
> → ☐ ☐ ☐ ☐ ☐ ☐ .

① me　　② her　　③ to
④ lent　　⑤ umbrella

08 대화의 빈칸에 들어갈 말로 알맞은 것은? |4점|

> A Did you move those heavy boxes alone?
> B No, I got my friends _____ me.

① help   ② helped   ③ helping
④ to help   ⑤ to helping

09 빈칸에 공통으로 들어갈 말로 알맞은 것은? |4점|

> • I will _____ a card for her birthday.
> • I sometimes _____ my sister cakes.
> • This song will _____ you calm.

① do   ② send   ③ make
④ keep   ⑤ have

10 빈칸에 들어갈 말로 알맞은 것을 <u>모두</u> 고르면? |3점|

> We helped him _____ dinner.

① cook   ② cooking   ③ cooked
④ to cook   ⑤ be cooked

11 밑줄 친 부분이 어법상 <u>틀린</u> 것은? |4점|

① You are so <u>friendly</u> to me.
② We found the building <u>easily</u>.
③ I consider these students <u>honestly</u>.
④ The little girl sings very <u>sweetly</u>.
⑤ You look <u>lovely</u> in that dress.

12 〈보기〉에서 빈칸에 들어갈 수 있는 동사의 개수는? |4점|

보기	ⓐ had	ⓑ let	ⓒ helped
	ⓓ wanted	ⓔ saw	ⓕ told

> She _____ me to join the soccer club.

① 1개   ② 2개   ③ 3개
④ 4개   ⑤ 5개

13 다음 중 어법상 옳은 문장은? |4점|

① The coach made him to a champion.
② I heard someone singing outside my window.
③ Kelly had her sister to wash the dishes.
④ Don't leave the door to open.
⑤ My parents didn't allow me read comic books.

14 (A)~(C)에 들어갈 말이 바르게 짝지어진 것은? |4점|

> • The moon shines (A) | bright / brightly |.
> • She had the fence (B) | paint / painted |.
> • I saw some boys (C) | running / to run | in the gym.

	(A)	(B)	(C)
①	bright	paint	running
②	bright	painted	to run
③	bright	painted	running
④	brightly	paint	to run
⑤	brightly	painted	running

15 문장의 형식이 〈보기〉와 같은 것은? |4점|

> 보기 Everyone called him a genius.

① She told us her secret.
② They consider him a liar.
③ The cat is sitting on the sofa.
④ The girl on the stage is very smart.
⑤ He showed me an interesting book.

고난도

16 밑줄 친 동사의 쓰임이 서로 같은 것은? |5점|

① He <u>got</u> me to drive his car.
　 The weather suddenly <u>got</u> cool.
② Do you <u>have</u> any worries?
　 I'll <u>have</u> my bike fixed tomorrow.
③ Please <u>keep</u> silent here.
　 A refrigerator <u>keeps</u> food fresh.
④ Can you <u>make</u> me a paper plane?
　 He always <u>makes</u> us do our best.
⑤ This game <u>looks</u> interesting.
　 He <u>looked</u> great in his tuxedo.

최신기출 고난도

17 어법상 틀린 부분을 <u>모두</u> 찾아 바르게 고친 것은? |5점|

> ⓐ Leaves turn red in fall.
> ⓑ He lent some money for me.
> ⓒ I expected Mary to pass the audition.
> ⓓ She had me to clean my room.

① ⓐ turn → turn to
② ⓐ turn → turn to, ⓑ for me → to me
③ ⓑ for me → to me, ⓒ to pass → pass
④ ⓑ for me → to me, ⓓ to clean → clean
⑤ ⓑ for me → to me, ⓒ to pass → pass,
　 ⓓ to clean → clean

18 주어진 문장을 3형식 문장으로 바꿔 쓰시오. |4점, 각 2점|

(1)
> I sent my mom a text message.

→ I sent _____.

(2)
> My dad made me spaghetti.

→ My dad made _____.

19 우리말과 일치하도록 괄호 안의 말을 바르게 배열하여 문장을 완성하시오. |4점|

> 그의 성공은 그의 친구들이 질투하게 만들었다.
> (his, made, jealous, friends)

→ His success _____.

[20-21] 다음 문장에서 어법상 <u>틀린</u> 부분을 찾아 바르게 고쳐 쓰시오. |4점, 각 2점|

20
> This blanket will keep you warmly.

_____ → _____

21
> Suddenly, I felt someone touched my shoulder.

_____ → _____

시험에 꼭 나오는 출제 포인트

Answers p. 4

출제 포인트 1 have been to(경험)와 have gone to(결과)를 헷갈리지 말자!

우리말과 일치하도록 빈칸에 알맞은 말을 쓰시오.

(1) 나는 우리 가족과 함께 부산에 두 번 가 봤다.

→ I _____ _____ to Busan with my family twice.

(2) 그는 런던에 가서 지금 여기에 없다.

→ He _____ _____ to London, so he is not here now.

출제 포인트 2 when, ago, yesterday 등 과거의 특정 시점을 나타내는 말은 현재완료와 함께 쓸 수 없다!

다음 중 어법상 틀린 문장은?

① I haven't seen this movie yet.
② He has been sick since last Friday.
③ We have lived in Seoul two years ago.
④ My brother broke the window yesterday.
⑤ My father has worked here for 10 years.

> **고득점 POINT** 의문사 when은 특정 시점을 묻는 말이므로 현재완료와 함께 쓸 수 없다.
>
> **다음 문장을 어법에 맞게 고쳐 쓰시오.**
>
> When have you finished cleaning your room?
> (너는 언제 네 방을 청소하는 것을 끝냈니?)
> → When _____ cleaning your room?

출제 포인트 3 과거에 일어난 두 가지 일 중 먼저 일어난 일을 과거완료로 쓴다는 것을 기억하자!

우리말과 일치하도록 괄호 안의 말을 이용하여 문장을 완성하시오.

그들이 역에 도착했을 때 기차는 이미 떠났다. (leave, get, already)

→ The train _____ when they _____ to the station.

출제 포인트 4 과거에 시작된 일이 현재까지 계속 진행되고 있을 때는 현재완료진행형을 쓴다!

두 문장을 한 문장으로 나타낼 때, 빈칸에 알맞은 말을 쓰시오.

> She started dancing at 5 p.m.
> She is still dancing now.

→ She _____ _____ _____
    since 5 p.m.

> **고득점 POINT** 「for + 기간」 vs. 「since + 시점」
>
> **괄호 안에서 알맞은 말을 고르시오.**
>
> (1) He has been watching TV (for / since) 2 p.m.
> (2) He has been watching TV (for / since) two hours.

[01-04] 다음 빈칸에 들어갈 말로 알맞은 것을 고르시오.
|8점, 각 2점|

01

Mr. Lee is our English teacher.
He _____ English to us since last year.

① teaches
② taught
③ has taught
④ had taught
⑤ will have taught

02

I _____ in London for two weeks before I came here.

① stay
② will stay
③ have stayed
④ had stayed
⑤ will have stayed

03

I _____ this camera for 10 years next year.

① have
② had
③ have had
④ had had
⑤ will have had

04

Look outside! It _____ since yesterday.

① is raining
② had rained
③ is been raining
④ has been raining
⑤ had been rained

05 밑줄 친 부분의 쓰임이 나머지와 <u>다른</u> 것은? |4점|

① I <u>have watched</u> the movie twice.
② <u>Have</u> you ever <u>talked</u> with Ms. Brown?
③ My uncle <u>has been</u> to Rome three times.
④ She <u>has</u> never <u>ridden</u> a horse.
⑤ <u>Have</u> you <u>done</u> your homework?

06 빈칸에 들어갈 말로 알맞은 것을 <u>모두</u> 고르면? |3점|

She has known about the surprise party _____.

① last Sunday
② yesterday
③ for two days
④ since last Sunday
⑤ three days ago

07 우리말과 일치하도록 할 때, 빈칸에 들어갈 말로 알맞은 것은? |4점|

나는 그때까지 외국인과 영어로 말해 본 적이 없었다.
→ I _____ to any foreigners in English until that time.

① don't speak
② didn't speak
③ never spoke
④ had never spoken
⑤ have never spoken

최신기출

08 다음 우리말을 영작할 때 쓰이지 <u>않는</u> 단어는? |4점|

나는 스페인에 가 본 적이 없다.

① to
② have
③ gone
④ been
⑤ never

09 대화의 빈칸에 들어갈 말로 알맞은 것은? |4점|

> A Jisu, where are you?
> B I'm coming into the theater now.
> A Hurry up! The movie _____.

① was been starting　　② is started
③ has just started　　④ had just started
⑤ will have started

10 빈칸에 알맞은 말이 순서대로 바르게 짝지어진 것은? |3점|

> • We have lived in this house _____ 20 years.
> • I have grown 10 cm _____ I entered middle school.

① in – for　　② for – in
③ since – for　　④ in – since
⑤ for – since

11 그림의 내용과 일치하도록 문장을 완성할 때, 빈칸에 알맞은 말이 순서대로 짝지어진 것은? |4점|

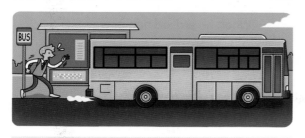

> When I _____ to the bus stop, the bus _____.

① get – had just left
② got – have just left
③ got – had just left
④ had got – just left
⑤ had got – had just left

12 다음 중 밑줄 친 부분이 어법상 옳은 것은? |5점|

① Have you ever <u>read</u> this novel?
② She <u>has bought</u> some books last week.
③ We <u>have finished</u> the work by tomorrow.
④ I failed the test because I <u>haven't studied</u> hard.
⑤ The snow <u>has already stopped</u> when I went out.

13 다음 두 문장을 한 문장으로 나타낼 때, 빈칸에 들어갈 말로 알맞은 것은? |4점|

> My grandmother started to live with us five years ago. She is still living with us.
> → My grandmother _____ with us for five years.

① started　　② is living
③ has started　　④ had lived
⑤ has been living

14 다음 중 현재완료를 <u>잘못</u> 사용한 학생은? |5점|

① 유빈: Sujin speaks Chinese fluently. She <u>has studied</u> it for five years.
② 민수: I know Mark well. He and I <u>have been</u> friends for a long time.
③ 은찬: I can go to Busan alone. I <u>have been</u> there several times.
④ 형준: I <u>have lost</u> my wallet yesterday, but I found it this morning.
⑤ 소민: I <u>have finished</u> all my homework! I'm free now!

15 빈칸에 been이 들어갈 수 <u>없는</u> 것은? |3점|

① I have _____ sick since last week.

② She has _____ practicing her speech for two hours.

③ Long time no see! How have you _____?

④ How long have you _____ working for this company?

⑤ My sister has _____ to Austria to study music, so she is not here.

16 어법상 옳은 문장을 <u>모두</u> 고른 것은? |4점|

> ⓐ When have you had a dog?
>
> ⓑ It has been cold since last Tuesday.
>
> ⓒ Did you ever been to New York?
>
> ⓓ How long have you watched TV?

① ⓐ   ② ⓑ   ③ ⓑ, ⓓ

④ ⓒ, ⓓ   ⑤ ⓐ, ⓑ, ⓓ

고난도

17 대화의 빈칸 ⓐ, ⓑ에 들어갈 말이 바르게 짝지어진 것은? |5점|

> A _____ ⓐ _____
>
> B Yes, I have seen Tom Cruise.
>
> A _____ ⓑ _____
>
> B I saw him at the airport last year.

① ⓐ Did you see a celebrity?
   ⓑ When did you see him?

② ⓐ Do you see a celebrity?
   ⓑ When do you see him?

③ ⓐ Did you ever see a celebrity?
   ⓑ When have you seen him?

④ ⓐ Have you ever seen a celebrity?
   ⓑ When did you see him?

⑤ ⓐ Have you ever seen a celebrity?
   ⓑ When have you seen him?

서술형

18 괄호 안의 말을 이용하여 완료시제의 문장으로 완성하시오. |6점, 각 2점|

(1) Ms. Baker _____ ill since last night. She will go to see a doctor. (be)

(2) Jonathan is writing a report now. He _____ his report by 2 o'clock. (finish)

(3) I recognized the man at once because I _____ him before. (meet)

최신기출

19 우리말과 일치하도록 〈보기〉에서 필요한 말을 골라 문장을 완성하시오. (중복 사용 가능) |6점, 각 3점|

보기	have	has	had
	been	gone	not	to

(1) 나는 뉴욕에 한 번 가 봤다.

→ I _____ _____ _____ New York once.

(2) 그가 집에 도착했을 때, 우리는 아직 저녁 식사를 하지 않았다.

→ When he arrived home, we _____ _____ _____ dinner yet.

20 어법상 <u>틀린</u> 부분을 찾아 바르게 고쳐 쓰시오. |3점|

> We have learning English since 2010.

_____ → _____

개념 우선 확인 | 밑줄 친 조동사의 의미 고르기

1 She <u>must</u> be hungry.
- ☐ 틀림없다
- ☐ 일지도 모른다

2 He <u>can't</u> be sick.
- ☐ 할 수 없다
- ☐ 일 리가 없다

3 You <u>may</u> use it.
- ☐ 해야 한다
- ☐ 해도 된다

A 괄호 안에서 알맞은 것을 고르시오.

1 They (don't have to / must not) smoke here. It is not allowed.

2 We are in a temple. We (ought not to / ought to not) make noise.

3 You (had not better / had better not) go out in this cold weather.

4 Joe had two hamburgers an hour ago. He (can't / must not) be hungry now.

B 괄호 안에서 나머지와 의미가 <u>다른</u> 하나를 고르시오.

1 He (can't / is not able to / may not) play the violin.

2 (Can / May / Should) I try on this shirt?

3 They (have to / ought to / would rather) go there as soon as possible.

4 You (must not / don't have to / should not) call him early in the morning.

C 〈보기〉에서 알맞은 말을 골라 대화를 완성하시오. (단, 한 번씩만 사용할 것)

보기   used to   don't have to   would rather

1 **A** Do you know that city well?
    B Yes, I _____ live there when I was a child.

2 **A** Would you like to go out for dinner?
    B No, I _____ stay home and watch TV.

3 **A** When does the movie begin?
    B It begins in two hours from now. We _____ hurry.

30초 완성 map

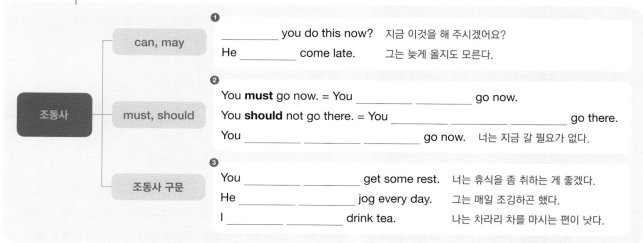

❶
_____ you do this now?   지금 이것을 해 주시겠어요?
He _____ come late.   그는 늦게 올지도 모른다.

❷
You **must** go now. = You _____ _____ go now.
You **should** not go there. = You _____ _____ _____ go there.
You _____ _____ _____ go now.   너는 지금 갈 필요가 없다.

❸
You _____ _____ get some rest.   너는 휴식을 좀 취하는 게 좋겠다.
He _____ _____ jog every day.   그는 매일 조깅하곤 했다.
I _____ _____ drink tea.   나는 차라리 차를 마시는 편이 낫다.

can, may

must, should

조동사

조동사 구문

조동사 + have p.p.

1 may (might) have p.p.

'~했을지도 모른다'라는 의미로 과거의 일에 대한 약한 추측을 나타낸다.

She	**may (might) have known**	your name.

그녀는 네 이름을 **알았을지도 모른다.**

Sue **may have lived** in Seoul for some time. She knows the city well.
Minho **might have won** the game. He practiced a lot every day.

> might have p.p.는 may have p.p.보다 약한 추측을 나타낸다.

2 must have p.p.

'~했던 게 틀림없다'라는 의미로 과거의 일에 대한 강한 추측을 나타낸다.

You	**must have made**	a big mistake.

너는 큰 실수를 **했던 게 틀림없다.**

They **must have seen** you at the mall yesterday.
He **must have been** hungry. He hadn't eaten anything all day.

3 can't have p.p.

'~했을 리가 없다'라는 의미로 과거의 일에 대한 강한 부정적 추측을 나타낸다.

He	**can't have been**	late.

그는 **늦었을 리가 없다.**

John **can't have made** this robot. He isn't interested in robots.
Mina **can't have called** you. She doesn't know your phone number.

4 should have p.p.

'~했어야 했다 (그런데 하지 않았다)'라는 의미로 과거의 일에 대한 후회나 유감을 나타낸다.

I	**should have gone**	there early.	나는 그곳에 일찍 **갔어야 했다.** (일찍 가지 않았다)
	shouldn't have gone		나는 그곳에 일찍 **가지 말았어야 했다.** (일찍 갔다)

We **should have studied** harder for the final exam.
(= We regret that we didn't study harder for the final exam.)
You **shouldn't have missed** the show.
(= I am sorry that you missed the show.)

시험
point

should have p.p.의 의미

should have p.p.는 '~해야 했다'라는 의미가 아니라 과거에 하지 않은 일에 대한 후회나 유감을 나타내는 것에 주의한다.

You <u>should have gone</u> to the concert yesterday. 너는 어제 콘서트에 (가야만 했다 / 갔어야 했는데 못 갔다).

개념 우선 확인 | 밑줄 친 말의 의미 고르기

1 He <u>must have gone</u> home.
- ☐ 갔어야 했다
- ☐ 갔던 게 틀림없다

2 You <u>should have called</u> me.
- ☐ 전화해야 한다
- ☐ 전화했어야 했다

3 She <u>can't have seen</u> it.
- ☐ 봤을 리가 없다
- ☐ 볼 수 없었다

A 괄호 안에서 알맞은 것을 고르시오.

1 We are late. We (must / should) have left earlier.

2 Henry has not arrived yet. He (may / can't) have missed the bus.

3 My mom looked tired. She must (be / have been) very busy all day.

4 He (can't / shouldn't) have drawn the picture. He is not good at drawing.

5 The musical was great. We (should / shouldn't) have watched it together.

B 우리말과 일치하도록 알맞은 조동사와 괄호 안의 말을 이용하여 문장을 완성하시오.

1 나는 그 컴퓨터를 샀어야 했는데, 그러지 않았다. (buy)
→ I _____ the computer, but I didn't.

2 그들이 어젯밤에 Charlie를 봤을지도 모른다. (see)
→ They _____ Charlie last night.

3 내 가장 친한 친구가 내 생일을 잊어버렸을 리가 없다. (forget)
→ My best friend _____ my birthday.

4 내가 이곳에 없는 동안 누군가 내 컴퓨터를 사용했던 게 틀림없다. (use)
→ Somebody _____ my computer while I was not here.

C 우리말과 일치하도록 할 때, 어법상 틀린 부분을 찾아 바르게 고쳐 쓰시오.

1 그가 너에게 거짓말했을 리가 없다. → He can't lied to you.

2 너는 그 영화를 봤어야 했다. → You should have saw the movie.

3 그녀는 시험에 통과했던 게 틀림없다. → She must have pass the exam.

30초 완성 map

조동사 + have p.p.				
❶ He _____ _____ _____ his homework.			그는 숙제를 했을지도 모른다.	
❷ He _____ _____ _____ his homework.			그는 숙제를 했던 게 틀림없다.	
❸ He _____ _____ _____ his homework.			그는 숙제를 했을 리가 없다.	
❹ He _____ _____ _____ his homework.			그는 숙제를 했어야 했다.	

서술형 대비 문장 쓰기

Answers p. 6

≡ 배열 영작 괄호 안의 말을 바르게 배열하기

01 너는 친구들에게 거짓말해서는 안 된다. (not, ought, lie, you, to)

→ _____ to your friends.

02 그는 진실을 알고 있었던 것이 틀림없지만 침묵을 지켰다. (the truth, he, known, must, have)

→ _____, but he kept silent.

03 나는 오늘 밤에 차라리 나가지 않는 게 낫겠다. (I, go out, rather, would, not)

→ _____ tonight.

04 이곳에 다리가 하나 있었다. (used, be, to, there, a bridge)

→ _____ here.

□ 빈칸 완성 괄호 안의 말을 이용하여 빈칸 완성하기

05 기차가 늦게 도착했기 때문에 우리는 일정을 바꿔야 했다. (have to, change)

→ We _____ our schedule because the train arrived late.

06 그곳은 따뜻하다. 너는 코트를 가져갈 필요가 없다. (have to, take)

→ It is warm there. You _____ your coat.

07 그의 발표는 완벽했다. 그는 그것에 많은 시간을 들였던 게 틀림없다. (must, spend)

→ His presentation was perfect. He _____ a lot of time on it.

08 그 배우는 이미 떠났다. 너는 더 일찍 왔어야 했다. (should, come)

→ The actor has already left. You _____ earlier.

✓ 오류 수정 어법에 맞게 문장 고쳐 쓰기

09 The job is dangerous, so you had not better do it.

→ The job is dangerous, so you _____.

10 When I was a child, I was used to go fishing with my dad.

→ When I was a child, I _____ with my dad.

11 I am very sleepy now. I should go to bed earlier last night.

→ I am very sleepy now. I _____ earlier last night.

12 The water was deep, so we have to wear a life jacket. *life jacket 구명조끼

→ The water was deep, so we _____ a life jacket.

시험에 꼭 나오는 출제 포인트

Answers p. 6

출제 포인트 1 조동사구의 부정에서 not의 위치에 주의하자!

우리말과 일치하도록 괄호 안의 말을 이용하여 문장을 완성하시오.

(1) 우리는 계획을 취소하지 않는 게 좋겠다. (had better)

→ We _____ _____ _____
cancel our plans.

(2) 너는 도서관에서 시끄럽게 하면 안 된다. (ought to)

→ You _____ _____ _____
make noise in the library.

> **고득점 POINT** would rather의 부정 형태
>
> **어법상 틀린 부분을 바르게 고쳐 문장을 완성하시오.**
> I wouldn't rather talk about the problem.
> → I _____ about the
> problem.

출제 포인트 2 조동사의 의미를 정확히 알아두자!

주어진 문장과 의미가 같도록 조동사를 이용하여 빈칸에 알맞은 말을 쓰시오.

(1) It is impossible that the story is true.

→ The story _____ _____ true.

(2) It is possible that Greg will be late for school.

→ Greg _____ _____ late for school.

출제 포인트 3 used to가 포함된 다양한 표현을 잘 구분하자!

괄호 안에서 알맞은 것을 고르시오.

We (used to / were used to) skate on the lake in winter.
(우리는 겨울에 호수에서 스케이트를 타곤 했다.)

출제 포인트 4 should have p.p.는 과거에 하지 않은 일에 대한 후회나 유감임을 알아두자!

우리말과 일치하도록 빈칸에 알맞은 말을 쓰시오.

지호는 영어를 더 열심히 공부했어야 했는데.

→ Jiho _____ _____ _____
English harder.

> **고득점 POINT** shouldn't have p.p.는 한 일에 대한 후회나
> 유감을 나타낸다.
>
> **두 문장의 의미가 같도록 알맞은 조동사를 사용하여 문장을 완성
> 하시오.**
> I regret that I ate so much last night.
> → I _____ _____ _____ so much last
> night.

[01-03] 다음 빈칸에 들어갈 말로 가장 알맞은 것을 고르시오.
|6점, 각 2점|

01

That man _____ be James. He went to London yesterday.

① may   ② must   ③ can't
④ should   ⑤ used to

02

There was no food in the house, so we _____ go grocery shopping this morning.

① can   ② must   ③ may
④ had to   ⑤ had better

03

Jessy hasn't come yet. She _____ have slept late in the morning.

① can   ② must   ③ should
④ can't   ⑤ would

04 밑줄 친 can의 의미가 〈보기〉와 같은 것은? |4점|

> 보기   You <u>can</u> take the book home if you want.

① She <u>can</u> swim fast.
② <u>Can</u> cats climb a tree?
③ It <u>can</u> get cold here at night.
④ <u>Can</u> I use your pen for a moment?
⑤ <u>Can</u> you take care of my dog tomorrow?

05 빈칸에 공통으로 들어갈 말로 가장 알맞은 것은? |3점|

• You _____ stop when the traffic light is red.
• My sister studied all night for an exam. She _____ be sleepy.

① can   ② will   ③ may
④ must   ⑤ should

06 밑줄 친 말을 의미가 같도록 바꿔 쓸 때, 알맞지 <u>않은</u> 것은?
|4점|

① <u>May</u> I use this computer?
   (→ Can)
② We <u>should</u> help each other.
     (→ ought to)
③ She <u>can</u> speak Korean.
     (→ is able to)
④ They <u>must not</u> be late.
      (→ don't have to)
⑤ You <u>may not</u> get on the bus with a drink.
     (→ can't)

07 다음 그림을 묘사하는 문장으로 알맞은 것은? |3점|

Before   Now

① He may have a beard.
② He must have a beard.
③ He used to have a beard.
④ He can't have had a beard.
⑤ He should have had a beard.   *beard 턱수염

08 두 문장의 의미가 같도록 할 때, 빈칸에 들어갈 말로 알맞은 것은? |3점|

> I regret that I didn't apologize to her.
> = I _____ have apologized to her.

① may   ② must
③ can't   ④ could
⑤ should

09 빈칸에 알맞은 말이 순서대로 바르게 짝지어진 것은? |4점|

> • I have been with him all day. He _____ the thief.
> • You did your best. Your parents _____ proud of you.

① must be – may be
② must be – can't be
③ can't be – must be
④ can't be – shouldn't be
⑤ must not be – may be

10 밑줄 친 ①~⑤ 중 대화의 흐름상 알맞지 <u>않은</u> 것은? |4점|

> A ①Can you help me with my homework?
> B I'm sorry, but I ②can't. I ③have to cook dinner.
> A You ④must not cook dinner. We ⑤can eat the leftover pizza from yesterday.
> B Awesome!
>
> *leftover 먹다 남은

11 다음 중 어법상 옳은 문장은? |4점|

① I would rather not go out today.
② You ought to not use a smartphone.
③ You had not better do that again.
④ I was used to play soccer after school.
⑤ There used to 60 students in a class.

12 다음 우리말을 영작할 때 필요하지 <u>않은</u> 단어는? |3점|

> 나는 내 휴대전화를 집에 두고 왔던 게 틀림없다.

① must   ② left   ③ leave
④ have   ⑤ cell phone

13 대화의 빈칸에 들어갈 말로 알맞은 것은? |4점|

> A I'm really hungry now.
>   I _____ lunch.
> B Let's go eat something.

① ate   ② have eaten
③ should ate   ④ should have eaten
⑤ shouldn't have eaten

14 어법상 <u>틀린</u> 부분을 찾아 바르게 고쳐 쓴 것은? |4점|

> The boy grew up in Kenya. He may not have saw snow in his country.

① may → should   ② saw → seen
③ have → had   ④ have saw → see
⑤ may not have → may have not

15 다음 중 영어 문장을 우리말로 잘못 옮긴 사람은?　|4점|

① I would rather wait here.
　　시원: 나는 차라리 이곳에서 기다리는 게 낫겠다.
② We don't have to get up early.
　　지윤: 우리는 일찍 일어날 필요가 없다.
③ This place used to be a bank.
　　성현: 이곳은 은행이었다.
④ You had better listen to your parents.
　　서준: 너는 부모님의 말씀을 듣는 게 좋겠다.
⑤ You ought not to believe everything he says.
　　경호: 너는 그의 말을 다 믿을 필요는 없다.

고난도

16 밑줄 친 부분이 문맥상 어색한 것은?　|5점|

① I feel so cold. I should have worn a coat.
② He got wet in the rain. He must have brought an umbrella with him.
③ He looks worried. He may have heard about the accident already.
④ She is a wise girl. She can't have done such a foolish thing.
⑤ Lisa was sleepy during the class. She shouldn't have stayed up late last night.

고난도

17 다음 글의 밑줄 친 부분 중, 어법상 틀린 것은?　|5점|

　　When I was young, my grandmother ①used to live near the East Sea. I ②would visit her every summer vacation. I ③used to enjoy swimming in the sea. There ④was used to be a big tree at the beach, so I ⑤would relax in the shade.

*shade 그늘

18 주어진 문장을 미래시제로 바꾼 문장을 완성하시오.
|6점, 각 3점|

(1) You can live free from worries.
→ You ＿＿＿＿＿＿＿＿＿＿＿ free from worries.
(2) You must stand in line to buy a ticket.
→ You ＿＿＿＿＿＿＿＿＿＿＿ to buy a ticket.

19 괄호 안의 말을 바르게 배열하여 문장을 완성하시오. |3점|

The rain has stopped. ＿＿＿＿＿＿＿

＿＿＿＿＿＿＿＿＿＿＿＿＿＿＿

(take, don't, you, an umbrella, to, have)

20 그림을 보고, 괄호 안의 말을 이용하여 남자아이와 여자아이에게 할 말을 완성하시오.　|4점, 각 2점|

(1) Tim, you ＿＿＿＿＿＿＿＿ garbage in the park. (had better, litter)　*litter 버리다
(2) Emma, you ＿＿＿＿＿＿＿＿ flowers in the park. (ought, pick)

개념 우선 확인 | **옳은 표현 고르기**

1 책을 읽고 싶다
- ☐ want to read a book
- ☐ to want read a book

2 가수가 되는 방법
- ☐ what to become a singer
- ☐ how to become a singer

3 (가지고) 쓸 펜
- ☐ a pen to write
- ☐ a pen to write with

A 괄호 안에서 알맞은 것을 고르시오.

1 His goal was (finish / to finish) the project in 10 days.

2 We need a small house to (stay / stay in) during our vacation.

3 I found (it / that) necessary to eat healthy food.

4 Can you tell me (whom to meet / to meet whom)?

B 〈보기〉에서 알맞은 말을 골라 「의문사＋to부정사」를 사용하여 문장을 완성하시오. (단, 한 번씩만 사용할 것)

보기	wear	go	visit	answer

1 This question is not easy. Can you show me ＿＿＿＿＿＿＿＿＿＿＿ it?

2 There are a lot of clothes in my closet, but I can't decide ＿＿＿＿＿＿＿＿＿＿＿.

3 This city has many interesting places. I don't know ＿＿＿＿＿＿＿＿＿＿＿ first.

4 Jane is very busy. I don't know ＿＿＿＿＿＿＿＿＿＿＿ her.

C 우리말과 일치하도록 괄호 안의 말을 이용하여 문장을 완성하시오.

1 물 없이 사는 것은 불가능하다. (impossible, live)

→ It is ＿＿＿＿＿＿＿＿＿＿＿ without water.

2 그는 이야기할 사람이 필요해서 내게 전화했다. (somebody, talk)

→ He called me because he needed ＿＿＿＿＿＿＿＿＿＿＿.

3 나는 그 경기에서 이길 것이라고 기대하지 않았다. (expect, win)

→ I didn't ＿＿＿＿＿＿＿＿＿＿＿ the game.

4 인터넷은 정보를 찾는 것을 쉽게 만들어 준다. (easy, search, it)

→ The Internet makes ＿＿＿＿＿＿＿＿＿＿＿ information.

30초 완성 map

to부정사

명사적 용법

❶
- **주어, 목적어, 보어 역할**
It is easy ＿＿＿＿ ＿＿＿＿ a cake. 케이크를 만드는 것은 쉽다.
- **의문사＋to부정사**
He didn't know ＿＿＿＿ ＿＿＿＿ ＿＿＿＿. 그는 무엇을 사야 할지 몰랐다.

형용사적 용법

❷
I need a friend to (play / play with). 나는 함께 놀 친구가 필요하다.

to부정사의 부사적 용법, to부정사의 시제·태

1 to부정사의 부사적 용법

목적	~하기 위해	He left early **to avoid** the heavy traffic.
감정의 원인	~해서, ~하게 되어	We were excited **to go** on a field trip.
결과	(…해서) ~하다	The boy grew up **to be** a lawyer.
판단의 근거	~하다니	You must be foolish **to fight** with him.
형용사 수식	~하기에	His lecture is difficult **to understand**.

❯ 목적의 의미를 명확히 나타내기 위해서 to부정사 앞에 in order 또는 so as를 쓰기도 한다.
He went to England **in order(so as) to learn** English.

2 to부정사의 시제

(1) to부정사의 시제가 문장의 시제와 같을 때: 「to + 동사원형」

Tom seems	**to like** you.	Tom은 너를 **좋아하는** 것 같다.
= It seems 현재	that Tom **likes** you. 현재	

(2) to부정사의 시제가 문장의 시제보다 앞설 때: 「to have + p.p.」

Tom seems	**to have liked** you.	Tom은 너를 **좋아했던** 것 같다.
= It seems 현재	that Tom **liked** you. 과거	

3 to부정사의 수동태

to부정사의 수동태는 「to be + p.p.」의 형태로 쓴다.

I am very happy	**to invite** her.	그녀를 초대함
	to be invited by her.	그녀에게 초대를 받음

I didn't expect **to be welcomed** by so many people.
There was no more work **to be done**, so we left.

시험
point

결과를 나타내는 to부정사

결과를 나타내는 to부정사는 보통 동사 다음에 and의 의미를 넣어 해석한다. 주로 grow up, live, awake 등의 동사와 함께 쓰인다.

I awoke **to find** a bird in my room. 나는 일어나**서** 내 방에서 새 한 마리를 **발견했다**.
(= I awoke *and found* a bird in my room.)

개념 우선 확인 | 밑줄 친 부분의 옳은 해석 고르기

1 I was happy <u>to see</u> you.
- ☐ 봐서
- ☐ 보기 위해

2 I went <u>to see</u> you.
- ☐ 봐서
- ☐ 보기 위해

3 You seem <u>to have been</u> happy.
- ☐ 행복한 것 같다
- ☐ 행복했던 것 같다

A 밑줄 친 부분을 우리말로 해석하시오.

1 They went to the park <u>to play badminton</u>.

2 I was glad <u>to meet you again</u>.

3 He must be rich <u>to live in that big house</u>.

4 My sister grew up <u>to be a popular pianist</u>.

B 두 문장의 의미가 같도록 빈칸에 알맞은 말을 쓰시오.

1 It seems that my parents understand my feelings.

→ My parents seem _____ my feelings.

2 It seems that he finished all the work.

→ He seems _____ all the work.

3 It seems that you changed your mind.

→ You seem _____ your mind.

C 〈보기〉에서 알맞은 말을 골라 **to**부정사를 사용하여 문장을 완성하시오. (단, 한 번씩만 사용할 것)

보기	borrow	eat	learn	choose

1 He came to my house _____ my camera.

2 Hangul is hard _____ in a short time.

3 She seems _____ lunch before she came here.

4 Ben was happy _____ for the soccer team.

30초 완성 map

to부정사

부사적 용법
He went to America **to study**. 그는 _____ 미국에 갔다.
I'm sorry **to be late**. _____ 미안해.
She grew up **to become a famous singer**. 그녀는 자라서 _____.

❷ 시제
She seems to _____ busy. 그녀는 바쁜 것 같다.
She seems to _____ _____ busy. 그녀는 바빴던 것 같다.

❸ 수동태
He is hoping **to be elected** president. 그는 대통령에 _____ 바라고 있다.

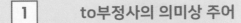

unit 3 to부정사의 의미상 주어, to부정사 구문

1 to부정사의 의미상 주어

to부정사의 행위의 주체를 to부정사의 의미상 주어라고 하며, to부정사 앞에 「for+목적격」의 형태로 쓴다.
사람의 성격이나 태도를 나타내는 형용사가 올 경우에는 「of+목적격」을 쓴다.

| It is easy | for him | to learn English. | 그가 영어를 배우는 것은 쉽다. |
| It is kind | of him | to help me. | 그가 나를 도와주다니 친절하다. |

> 의미상 주어로 「of+목적격」을 쓰는 형용사
> kind, nice, wise, foolish, smart, careful, rude, polite 등

2 to부정사 구문

(1) 「**too**+형용사/부사+**to부정사**」: '너무 ~해서 …할 수 없는'이라는 의미로 「so+형용사/부사+that+주어+can't+동사원형」으로 바꿔 쓸 수 있다.

| | He is | **too** young | **to travel** alone. |
| → | He is | **so** young | **that** he **can't travel** alone. |

> to부정사의 의미상 주어가 있는 경우에는 의미상 주어가 that절의 주어가 된다. that절에서 동사의 목적어가 필요한 경우에는 목적어를 꼭 써야 하는 것에 유의한다.

| | This box is | **too** heavy | for me **to carry**. |
| → | This box is | **so** heavy | **that I can't carry** it. |

(2) 「형용사/부사+**enough**+**to부정사**」: '~할 만큼 충분히 …한/하게'라는 의미로 「so+형용사/부사+that+주어+can+동사원형」으로 바꿔 쓸 수 있다.

| | My bag is | big **enough** | **to hold** five books. |
| → | My bag is | **so** big | **that** it **can hold** five books. |

> 주절의 시제가 과거인 경우에는 that절에 could를 쓴다.

| | The shirt **was** | cheap **enough** | for him **to buy**. |
| → | The shirt **was** | **so** cheap | **that** he **could buy** it. |

주의 enough는 형용사나 부사 다음에 위치한다.

시험
point

too ~ to부정사 구문을 so ~ that … can't 구문으로 바꿀 때 주의할 점

① too를 so로 바꾸기 ② 의미상 주어가 있으면 that절의 주어로!
③ 주절의 시제가 과거이면 couldn't로!
④ 동사의 목적어가 필요하면 꼭 써주기

  The problem was **too** difficult to solve.

→ The problem was **so** difficult **that I couldn't solve** .
    ①   ②   ③   ④

1 내가 하기 힘들다
- ☐ difficult for me to do
- ☐ difficult of me to do

2 네가 돕다니 친절하다
- ☐ nice for you to help
- ☐ nice of you to help

3 너무 바빠서 갈 수 없다
- ☐ too busy to go
- ☐ busy enough to go

A 괄호 안에서 알맞은 것을 고르시오.

1 It was foolish (for / of) me to buy such a useless thing.

2 It is necessary (for / of) us to go and help them now.

3 It was wise (for / of) her not to believe the rumor.

4 It is important (for / of) them to speak two foreign languages.

B 밑줄 친 부분을 어법에 맞게 고쳐 쓰시오.

1 It wasn't nice <u>for them</u> to leave without saying goodbye.

2 I was <u>so sick</u> to go to school yesterday.

3 His voice is <u>enough loud</u> for people in the back to hear.

4 The car was so expensive that he <u>couldn't buy</u>.

C 두 문장의 의미가 같도록 빈칸에 알맞은 말을 쓰시오.

1 I was so hungry that I couldn't concentrate during class.

→ I was ＿＿＿＿＿ ＿＿＿＿＿ ＿＿＿＿＿ ＿＿＿＿＿ during class.

2 The room is so big that everyone can fit in it.

→ The room is ＿＿＿＿＿ ＿＿＿＿＿ ＿＿＿＿＿ ＿＿＿＿＿ ＿＿＿＿＿

＿＿＿＿＿ in.

3 The coffee is too hot for me to drink.

→ The coffee is ＿＿＿＿＿ ＿＿＿＿＿ ＿＿＿＿＿ ＿＿＿＿＿ ＿＿＿＿＿

＿＿＿＿＿ ＿＿＿＿＿.

30초 완성 map

to부정사

의미상 주어

❶ It is impossible ＿＿＿＿＿ ＿＿＿＿＿ ＿＿＿＿＿ ＿＿＿＿＿ this box. (carry)
네가 이 상자를 나르는 것은 불가능하다.

It is nice ＿＿＿＿＿ ＿＿＿＿＿ ＿＿＿＿＿ ＿＿＿＿＿ this box for me. (carry)
네가 나를 위해 이 상자를 나르다니 친절하구나.

to부정사 구문

❷ It is ＿＿＿＿＿ ＿＿＿＿＿ for us ＿＿＿＿＿ ＿＿＿＿＿ outside now.
→ It is **so** cold **that** we **can't go** outside now.

She is ＿＿＿＿＿ ＿＿＿＿＿ ＿＿＿＿＿ ＿＿＿＿＿ this book.
→ She is **so** smart **that** she **can understand** this book.

배열 영작 괄호 안의 말을 바르게 배열하기

01 그들은 살 집을 찾는 중이다. (live, a house, in, to)

→ They are looking for _____.

02 나에게 우산을 빌려주다니 그는 매우 친절했다. (me, lend, him, of, to)

→ It was very kind _____ an umbrella.

03 그는 어디로 가야 할지 정말 알지 못했다. (go, know, to, where)

→ He really didn't _____.

04 나는 그녀로부터 선물을 받아서 매우 기뻤다. (a present, glad, to, very, get)

→ I was _____ from her.

문장 전환 두 문장의 의미가 같도록 문장 바꿔 쓰기 (부정형은 축약형으로 쓸 것)

05 I don't know how I should turn on this machine.

→ I don't know _____ _____ _____ _____ this machine.

06 It seems that he lived in France when he was a child.

→ He seems _____ _____ _____ _____ France when he was a child.

07 He was too busy to call me yesterday.

→ He was _____ that _____ _____ _____ me yesterday.

08 She spoke so slowly that everyone could understand her.

→ She spoke _____ _____ _____ _____ to understand her.

빈칸 완성 괄호 안의 말을 이용하여 빈칸 완성하기

09 너는 이 일을 지금 당장 끝낼 필요가 있다. (necessary, finish, you)

→ It is _____ this work right away.

10 수민이는 내 비밀에 대해 뭔가를 알고 있는 것 같다. (seem, know)

→ Sumin _____ something about my secret.

11 그는 혼자 여행할 만큼 충분히 나이가 들지 않았다. (enough, old, travel)

→ He is not _____ alone.

12 이 책은 너무 어려워서 그녀가 읽을 수 없다. (too, difficult, read, her)

→ This book is _____.

시험에 꼭 나오는 출제 포인트

Answers p. 8

출제 포인트 ① to부정사의 의미상 주어 앞에 for를 쓰는 경우와 of를 쓰는 경우를 잘 구분하자!

우리말과 일치하도록 빈칸에 알맞은 말을 쓰시오.

(1) 그가 화가 난 것은 당연했다.

→ It was natural _____ _____ to get angry.

(2) 내가 너를 믿다니 어리석었다.

→ It was foolish _____ _____ to trust you.

출제 포인트 ② 「형용사 / 부사 + enough + to부정사」에서 enough의 위치에 주의하자!

우리말과 일치하도록 괄호 안의 말을 바르게 배열하시오.

> 이 강은 수영할 만큼 충분히 깊다.
> (enough, swim, deep, in, to)

→ This river is _____.

> **고득점 POINT** so ~ that 구문을 enough to로 바꿀 때 형용사나 부사의 위치에 주의한다.
>
> **두 문장의 의미가 같도록 빈칸에 알맞은 말을 쓰시오.**
>
> It is so warm that we can wear shorts today.
> → It is _____ _____ for us _____ _____ shorts today.

출제 포인트 ③ to부정사 구문을 so ~ that 구문으로 바꿀 때 that절의 시제와 목적어에 주의하자!

두 문장의 의미가 같도록 빈칸에 알맞은 말을 쓰시오.

The shirt was too expensive for me to buy.

→ The shirt was so expensive that I _____ _____ _____.

> **고득점 POINT** so ~ that 구문에서 that절에 not이 있으면 too ~ to 구문으로 바꿔 쓴다.
>
> **주어진 문장을 의미가 같도록 to부정사 구문으로 바꿔 쓰시오.**
>
> The room is so dark that I can't see anything.
> → The room is _____ anything.

출제 포인트 ④ 「to have + p.p.」는 문장의 시제보다 앞서 일어난 일임에 주의하자!

두 문장의 의미가 같도록 할 때, 빈칸에 알맞은 것은?

> She seems to have loved you.
> = It seems that she _____ you.

① love   ② loves   ③ loved
④ is loving   ⑤ had loved

유형	문항수	배점	점수
객관식	17	58	
서술형	10	42	

[01-03] 다음 빈칸에 들어갈 말로 알맞은 것을 고르시오.

|6점, 각 2점|

01

It is not easy _____ money.

① save ② saves ③ saved
④ to save ⑤ to saved

02

Jack is looking for someone to _____.

① play ② played ③ playing
④ play with ⑤ playing with

03

Mia seems to _____ sick last week.

① be ② have ③ had
④ had be ⑤ have been

04 우리말과 일치하도록 할 때, 빈칸에 들어갈 말로 알맞은 것은?

|4점|

나는 그의 생일 파티에 초대받을 것이라고 기대하지 않았다.

→ I didn't expect _____ to his birthday party.

① inviting ② to invite
③ being invited ④ to be invited
⑤ to be inviting

[05-06] 밑줄 친 부분의 쓰임이 나머지와 다른 것을 고르시오.

|6점, 각 3점|

05 ① To listen to others is important.
② I want to travel around the world.
③ His job is to drive the school bus.
④ I have a lot of things to do today.
⑤ It is impossible to live without water.

06 ① Her handwriting is hard to read.
② I don't have many clothes to wear.
③ There are many interesting places to visit.
④ The travelers wanted something cold to drink.
⑤ I need some friends to talk with when I am lonely.

07 빈칸에 들어갈 말이 나머지와 다른 것은? |3점|

① The essay is too difficult _____ us to read.
② It is wise _____ him to save money for the future.
③ It is dangerous _____ you to ride a bike without a helmet.
④ It is not easy _____ me to learn foreign languages.
⑤ There are several ways _____ you to prepare for the interview.

[08-09] 두 문장의 의미가 같도록 할 때, 빈칸에 들어갈 말로 알맞은 것을 고르시오. |8점, 각 4점|

08

The movie was too scary for us to watch.
= The movie was so scary that we
_____.

① can't watch
② could watch
③ could watch it
④ couldn't watch
⑤ couldn't watch it

09

It seems that she had a good time.
= She seems to _____ a good time.

① have
② has
③ had
④ have had
⑤ had had

10 빈칸에 들어갈 말로 알맞지 않은 것은? |3점|

It is _____ for them to understand the rules.

① easy
② smart
③ difficult
④ impossible
⑤ necessary

11 주어진 문장을 enough to를 이용하여 바꿔 쓸 때, 다섯 번째로 오는 단어는? |4점|

My sister is so strong that she can move the heavy table.

① to
② move
③ strong
④ enough
⑤ table

12 빈칸에 공통으로 들어갈 말로 알맞은 것은? |3점|

• Is _____ a good idea to study early in the morning?
• I think _____ impossible to master a foreign language in a year.

① it
② this
③ that
④ what
⑤ which

13 대화의 빈칸에 들어갈 말로 알맞은 것은? |3점|

A What are you doing?
B I want some *dalgona*, but I don't know _____ make it.
A I advise you to look it up on the Internet.

① how to
② what to
③ when to
④ whom to
⑤ where to

14 다음 중 밑줄 친 부분을 잘못 고친 것은? |5점|

ⓐ She seems to live here last year.
ⓑ He was excited to choose the winner.
ⓒ Can I get a clean piece of paper to write?
ⓓ It is wise for you to accept my offer.
ⓔ The sneakers were cheap enough for me to buy them.

① ⓐ → to have lived
② ⓑ → to have chosen
③ ⓒ → to write on
④ ⓓ → of you to accept
⑤ ⓔ → to buy

15 빈칸에 알맞은 말이 순서대로 바르게 짝지어진 것은? |4점|

- He seems to _____ seen the accident.
- They seem to _____ satisfied with the presents.

① be – be ② be – have
③ have – be ④ have – have
⑤ had – have

16 다음 중 두 문장의 의미가 서로 다른 것은? |4점|

① It seems that Tom was sick.
= Tom seemed to be sick.
② To stay home all day is boring.
= It is boring to stay home all day.
③ I can't decide what to eat for lunch.
= I can't decide what I should eat for lunch.
④ This song is easy enough for me to sing.
= This song is so easy that I can sing it.
⑤ The chair was too heavy for him to move.
= The chair was so heavy that he couldn't move it.

고난도

17 다음 중 어법상 틀린 문장의 개수는? |5점|

ⓐ I was trying hard to not laugh out loud.
ⓑ To plant a lot of trees are good for the earth.
ⓒ She promised in order to do her best in the match.
ⓓ Please let me know when turn right.
ⓔ All the students were excited to listen to her beautiful song.

① 1개 ② 2개 ③ 3개 ④ 4개 ⑤ 5개

서 술 형

[18-20] 두 문장의 의미가 같도록 to부정사를 이용한 문장으로 완성하시오. |9점, 각 3점|

18
The pot was so hot that we couldn't touch it.

→ The pot was _____ for us _____.

19
I don't know what I should say to make you happy.

→ I don't know _____ to make you happy.

20
It seems that Matt enjoyed skiing.

→ Matt seems _____.

고난도

21 어법상 틀린 두 곳을 찾아 바르게 고쳐 문장을 다시 쓰시오. |5점|

This book is enough easy for me to read it.

→ _____

개념 우선 확인 | 밑줄 친 부분의 옳은 해석 고르기

1 Taking a shower, he sang loudly.
- ☐ 샤워를 해서
- ☐ 샤워를 하면서

2 Being busy, he couldn't go there.
- ☐ 바빠서
- ☐ 바쁜 동안

A 괄호 안에서 알맞은 것을 고르시오.

1 (Play / Playing) soccer with his friends, he hurt his leg.

2 (Be / Being) hungry, they stopped for lunch at a restaurant.

3 (Not feeling / Feeling not) well, Tim went to bed early after dinner.

4 (Being / It being) Sam's birthday soon, we are planning a surprise party.

B 밑줄 친 부사절을 분사구문으로 바꿔 쓰시오. (단, 접속사는 생략할 것)

1 After we reached the top of the mountain, we took this picture.

→ _____, we took this picture.

2 As I don't have enough money, I can't buy my mom a birthday present.

→ _____, I can't buy my mom a birthday present.

3 While he talked on the phone, he continued playing the computer game.

→ _____, he continued playing the computer game.

C 우리말과 일치하도록 괄호 안의 말을 이용하여 문장을 완성하시오.

1 샌드위치를 먹으면서 그녀는 기차를 기다렸다. (eat, a sandwich)

→ _____ _____ _____, she waited for the train.

2 프랑스어를 알지 못해서 나는 그 책을 읽을 수 없다. (know, French)

→ _____ _____ _____, I can't read the book.

3 날씨가 좋아서 우리는 산책을 했다. (the weather, nice)

→ _____ _____ _____ _____, we took a walk.

30초 완성 map

분사구문

형태

❶
As I knew the answer, I raised my hand.

→ _____ the answer, I raised my hand.

As I didn't have a cell phone, I couldn't call you.

→ _____ _____ a cell phone, I couldn't call you.

As it was Sunday, I stayed home.

→ _____ _____ Sunday, I stayed home.

의미

❷
Listening to music, I did my homework. _____ 나는 숙제를 했다.

Having a lot of work to do, she can't come. _____ 그녀는 올 수 없다.

unit 3 다양한 분사구문

1 완료형 분사구문

부사절의 시제가 주절의 시제보다 앞선 경우에 「having+p.p.」의 형태로 쓴다.

과거 ~~As he~~ played the game until 2 a.m.,	현재 he is very tired now.
→ **Having played** the game until 2 a.m.,	
새벽 2시까지 게임을 해서	그는 지금 매우 피곤하다.

2 수동형 분사구문

부사절이 수동태인 경우 「being+p.p.」의 형태로 쓰고, 이때 being은 주로 생략하고 과거분사로 시작한다.

~~As he~~ was surrounded by many fans,	the actor felt happy.
→ **(Being) Surrounded** by many fans,	
많은 팬들에게 둘러 싸여서	그 배우는 행복했다.

▷ 부사절의 시제가 주절보다 앞선 경우 「having been+p.p.」를 쓰는데, 이때 having been도 주로 생략한다.

~~Because it~~ was written 100 years ago, the letter is hard to read.
→ **(Having been) Written** 100 years ago, the letter is hard to read.

3 with+(대)명사+분사

'~가 …하면서, ~가 …한 채로'라는 의미로, (대)명사와 분사의 관계가 능동·진행이면 현재분사를, 수동·완료이면 과거분사를 쓴다.

She sat	with	her eyes	shining.	눈을 반짝이며
		her arms	crossed.	팔짱을 낀 채로

She looked at me **with tears running** down her face.
The car was parked here **with its window** already **broken**.

4 숙어처럼 쓰이는 분사구문

frankly speaking	솔직히 말해서	speaking of	~에 관해 말하자면
generally speaking	일반적으로 말해서	judging from	~으로 판단하건대
strictly speaking	엄밀히 말해서	considering	~을 고려하면

Frankly speaking, I didn't like her idea.
Considering his age, he plays the piano very well.

시험 point

분사구문의 능동과 수동 구분

분사구문이 능동인지 수동인지는 주절의 주어와의 관계를 살펴 판단한다.

1 (Writing / Written) in simple English, **the book** is easy to understand.
2 (Writing / Written) an email in English, **she** looked up a word in the dictionary.

개념 우선 확인 | 옳은 표현 고르기

1 이모 손에 길러져서
☐ raising by my aunt
☐ raised by my aunt

2 팔짱을 낀 채로
☐ with his arms crossing
☐ with his arms crossed

3 날씨를 고려하면
☐ considering the weather
☐ considered the weather

A 괄호 안에서 알맞은 것을 고르시오.

1 (Forgotten / Having forgotten) to bring my umbrella, I ran in the rain.

2 (Seeing / Seen) from the sky, the river looked like a huge snake.

3 She was lying on the bed with her baby (sleeping / slept) next to her.

4 Generally (speaking / spoken), it is not easy to master a foreign language.

5 (Having not read / Not having read) the book, I don't know the story.

B 우리말과 일치하도록 괄호 안의 말을 이용하여 분사구문을 완성하시오.

1 런던에 살았었기 때문에 그는 영어를 유창하게 말할 수 있다. (live)

→ _____ _____ in London, he can speak English fluently.

2 방 안에 혼자 남겨졌을 때 그녀는 울기 시작했다. (leave, alone)

→ _____ _____ in the room, she began to cry.

3 그녀의 얼굴 표정으로 판단하건대 Jenny는 여기에 오고 싶지 않았다. (judge)

→ _____ _____ her facial expression, Jenny didn't want to come here.

4 겨울이 다가오면서, 우리는 스키를 타러 가기로 계획했다. (with, winter, come)

→ _____ _____ _____ on, we planned to go skiing.

C 밑줄 친 부분을 어법에 맞게 고쳐 쓰시오.

1 <u>Finished</u> the project, we will soon take a very long vacation.

2 <u>Shocking</u> by the accident, I couldn't do anything.

3 <u>Not satisfying</u> with the results, he decided to do it again.

30초 완성 map

분사구문

완료형 분사구문 ❶ _____ already _____ the movie, he knew the story. (watch)
이미 그 영화를 봐서 그는 줄거리를 알았다.

수동형 분사구문 ❷ _____ at the news, I couldn't say a word. (surprise)
그 소식에 놀라서 나는 한마디도 할 수 없었다.

with+ (대)명사+분사 ❸ She sat on the chair _____ her legs _____ . (cross)
그녀는 다리를 꼰 채로 의자에 앉아 있었다.

서술형 대비 문장 쓰기

Answers p. 12

≡ 배열 영작 괄호 안의 말을 바르게 배열하기 (필요한 경우, 형태를 바꿀 것)

01 그 의사는 나왔을 때 매우 지쳐 보였다. (tire, looked, really)

→ When the doctor came out, she _____.

02 그는 눈을 감은 채로 음악을 듣고 있었다. (with, close, his eyes)

→ He was listening to music _____.

03 그녀는 주로 유명한 작가들이 쓴 책들을 읽는다. (write, books, famous authors, by)

→ She usually reads _____.

04 엄마는 우리들이 노는 것을 보면서 벤치에 앉아 계셨다. (play, watch, us)

→ Mom sat on the bench _____.

↻ 문장 전환 밑줄 친 부사절을 분사구문으로 바꿔 쓰기

05 As he didn't know how to start the machine, he called for help.

→ _____, he called for help.

06 While I was riding a roller coaster, I dropped my phone.

→ _____, I dropped my phone.

07 Because it was rainy, nobody wanted to go out.

→ _____, nobody wanted to go out.

08 Since she was confused about her life, she didn't know what to do.

→ _____, she didn't know what to do.

✓ 오류 수정 어법에 맞게 문장 고쳐 쓰기

09 The teacher surround by children looks very happy.

→ _____ looks very happy.

10 He stood up quickly with his hands raising over his head.

→ He stood up quickly _____ over his head.

11 Having not study hard, Jin was worried about the test.

→ _____, Jin was worried about the test.

12 While stayed in Seoul, Tom visited many interesting places.

→ _____, Tom visited many interesting places.

시험에 나오는 출제 포인트

Answers p. 12

출제 포인트 1 수식하는 명사와 능동의 관계이면 현재분사를, 수동의 관계이면 과거분사를 쓴다!

밑줄 친 부분의 쓰임이 어법상 틀린 것은?

① I bought jeans <u>made</u> in China.
② I saw a baby <u>sleeping</u> in the bed.
③ People <u>lived</u> in this town usually live long.
④ Some of the girls <u>invited</u> to the party didn't come.
⑤ Children tried to find the <u>hidden</u> treasures.

> **고득점 POINT** 주어가 분사구의 수식을 받는 경우, 동사는 주어에 일치시켜야 한다.
>
> **괄호 안에서 알맞은 것을 고르시오.**
> The man wearing glasses (is / are) my English teacher.

출제 포인트 2 감정을 느끼게 만들면 현재분사, 감정을 느끼면 과거분사임을 알아두자!

괄호 안의 말을 알맞은 형태로 바꿔 빈칸에 쓰시오.

(1) The movie I saw yesterday was very _____. (interest)

(2) His behavior makes me _____ to be his classmate. (embarrass)

출제 포인트 3 -ing 형태가 나오면 현재분사인지 동명사인지 그 쓰임에 주의하자!

밑줄 친 부분의 쓰임이 나머지와 다른 것은?

① I saw her <u>running</u> through the crowd.
② We heard him <u>calling</u> his students.
③ She caught the ball <u>flying</u> toward her face.
④ There were lots of people <u>crying</u> at the news.
⑤ Instead of <u>buying</u> a pair of shoes, I bought a jacket.

출제 포인트 4 분사구문의 형태를 잘 기억하자!

어법상 틀린 부분을 찾아 바르게 고쳐 쓰시오.

(1) Walked down the street, I sang a song.

_____ → _____

(2) Writing in easy Korean, the book is good for foreigners.

_____ → _____

> **고득점 POINT** 분사구문의 부정 형태
>
> **밑줄 친 부분을 분사구문으로 바꿔 쓰시오.**
> As I have not met him before, I don't know him well.
> → _____,
> I don't know him well.

[01-03] 다음 빈칸에 들어갈 말로 알맞은 것을 고르시오.
|6점, 각 2점|

01

We lay on the grass and looked at the _____ stars last night.

① shine ② shone ③ shined
④ shining ⑤ to shine

02

There were no seats _____ because I was late.

① leave ② left ③ leaving
④ leaves ⑤ to leaving

03

_____ on a hill, the hotel has a beautiful view.

① Locate ② Located
③ Locating ④ Have locating
⑤ Been located

04 밑줄 친 부분의 쓰임이 나머지와 다른 것은? |3점|

① Her hobby is collecting stickers.
② The man is drinking coffee now.
③ I read an interesting book last night.
④ Do you know the boy playing soccer over there?
⑤ People looked at the lady wearing a red dress.

05 밑줄 친 부분의 쓰임이 어법상 옳은 것은? |4점|

① I felt so tiring after the trip.
② The final match was excited.
③ He was surprising at the news.
④ Why do you look so boring?
⑤ The news that she died was very shocking.

06 다음 우리말을 영작할 때, 알맞지 않은 것은? |3점|

① 낙엽 : the fallen leaves
② 깨진 유리 : the broken glass
③ 떠오르는 태양 : the rising sun
④ 영어로 쓰인 소설 : a novel written in English
⑤ 인도에서 쓰는 언어들 : the languages speaking in India

고난도

07 괄호 안의 동사를 알맞은 형태로 바꿀 때, 같은 형태인 것끼리 바르게 짝지어진 것은? |5점|

ⓐ He has a lovely son (call) Dave.
ⓑ She kept me (wait) in her room.
ⓒ Who is the girl (play) the piano?
ⓓ The sound of rain makes me feel (relax).
ⓔ I had an (amaze) experience in Paris.

① ⓐ, ⓒ - ⓑ, ⓓ, ⓔ
② ⓐ, ⓓ - ⓑ, ⓒ, ⓔ
③ ⓐ, ⓔ - ⓑ, ⓒ, ⓓ
④ ⓐ, ⓑ, ⓒ - ⓓ, ⓔ
⑤ ⓐ, ⓓ, ⓔ - ⓑ, ⓒ

08 우리말과 일치하도록 괄호 안의 말을 배열할 때, 다섯 번째로 오는 단어는? |3점|

> 소파에 누워있는 고양이를 봐.
> (the cat, look, on, lying, at, the sofa)

① look   ② sofa   ③ on
④ cat   ⑤ lying

09 밑줄 친 부분이 어법상 옳은 문장끼리 짝지어진 것은? |5점|

> ⓐ I tried hard to open the <u>locked</u> door.
> ⓑ She plans to buy a <u>using</u> car.
> ⓒ I fixed the bike <u>damaged</u> during the race.
> ⓓ Ben found himself in an <u>embarrassing</u> situation.
> ⓔ After <u>eaten</u> dinner, we cleaned the table together.

① ⓐ, ⓑ   ② ⓑ, ⓒ   ③ ⓐ, ⓑ, ⓓ
④ ⓐ, ⓒ, ⓓ   ⑤ ⓐ, ⓒ, ⓓ, ⓔ

10 빈칸에 알맞은 말이 순서대로 바르게 짝지어진 것은? |4점|

> Our fence was _____ last week. But I found it _____ by someone this morning.

① broken – fixed
② broken – fixing
③ to break – fixed
④ breaking – fixed
⑤ breaking – fixing

11 밑줄 친 부분을 부사절로 바꿀 때, 빈칸에 알맞은 것은? |3점|

> <u>Being an only child</u>, I often feel lonely.
> → _____ I am an only child, I often feel lonely.

① If   ② As   ③ When
④ While   ⑤ After

12 밑줄 친 부분을 분사구문으로 바르게 바꾼 것은? |3점|

> <u>Since I didn't have my umbrella</u>, I got wet.

① Not have my umbrella
② Having not my umbrella
③ Not having my umbrella
④ Didn't having my umbrella
⑤ Not having been had my umbrella

[13-14] 우리말과 일치하도록 할 때, 빈칸에 알맞은 말을 고르시오. |8점, 각 4점|

13
> _____, I didn't make a mistake.
> (엄밀히 말해서, 나는 실수하지 않았다.)

① Spoken strictly   ② Strictly spoken
③ Strict speaking   ④ Speaking strictly
⑤ Strictly speaking

14
> He listened to the radio with _____.
> (그는 다리를 꼰 채로 라디오를 들었다.)

① his legs crossed   ② crossing his legs
③ crossed his legs   ④ his legs crossing
⑤ his crossing legs

15 밑줄 친 부분을 부사절로 바꿀 때, 알맞지 <u>않은</u> 것은? |4점|

① Getting home, I was very hungry.
  (→ When I got home)
② Having nothing to eat, we ate out.
  (→ Because we had nothing to eat)
③ She got in the car, waving to us.
  (→ as she was waving to us)
④ Walking on the street, I was talking on the phone.
  (→ Since I walked on the street)
⑤ Listening to music, he made lunch.
  (→ As he listened to music)

고난도

16 밑줄 친 부분이 어법상 틀린 것은? |5점|

① <u>Being tired</u>, we couldn't move at all.
② <u>Not chosen</u> for the national team, he was disappointed.
③ <u>Lived in Busan now</u>, she knows the city well.
④ <u>Having finished the test</u>, I had fun with my friends all weekend.
⑤ <u>The weather being bad</u>, we had to stay in the hotel all day.

최신기출

17 밑줄 친 ⓐ~ⓔ 중 어법상 틀린 것을 찾아 바르게 고친 사람은? |4점|

I visited Ann's house last week. She lives in a large house ⓐ<u>made</u> of wood. She has a little dog ⓑ<u>named</u> Simon. I could hear him ⓒ<u>barking</u> when I got there. I was ⓓ<u>amazed</u> at her garden ⓔ<u>filling</u> with flowers.

① 예빈: ⓐ made → making
② 혜미: ⓑ named → naming
③ 현진: ⓒ barking → barked
④ 지민: ⓓ amazed → amazing
⑤ 재호: ⓔ filling → filled

서술형

18 빈칸에 들어갈 말을 〈보기〉에서 골라 알맞은 형태로 쓰시오. |3점, 각 1점|

보기	write	serve	sit

(1) The girl _____ on the bench is my sister.
(2) My dad bought me a book _____ in Spanish.
(3) The soup _____ at this restaurant tastes good.

고난도

19 어법상 틀린 문장을 두 개 골라 기호를 쓰고, 바르게 고쳐 문장을 다시 쓰시오. |5점|

ⓐ The movie was so bored that I fell asleep.
ⓑ Henry seemed to have some interesting news.
ⓒ She looked disappointed when she heard her test score.
ⓓ I can't read the map because it is confused.

(   ) → _____

_____

(   ) → _____

_____

20 다음 대화에서 어법상 틀린 부분을 찾아 바르게 고쳐 쓰시오. |4점|

A How was your trip to the museum?
B It was great! I saw a picture drawing by Leonardo da Vinci.

_____ → _____

개념 우선 확인 | 옳은 문장 고르기

1 음악이 연주되는 중이다.
- ☐ The music is playing.
- ☐ The music is being played.

2 그 탑은 여기서 보인다.
- ☐ The tower can see here.
- ☐ The tower can be seen here.

3 새 책이 출간되었다.
- ☐ A new book has released.
- ☐ A new book has been released.

A 괄호 안에서 알맞은 것을 고르시오.

1 The thief (has not been / has not) caught yet.

2 This puzzle (can't solve / can't be solved) by anyone.

3 The national treasure (found / was found) 10 years ago.

4 When I went to that village, a large wall was (been / being) painted.

B 밑줄 친 부분을 어법에 맞게 고쳐 쓰시오.

1 A new stadium <u>will build</u> in Seoul next year.

2 A beautiful song <u>is singing</u> on the stage.

3 The accident <u>was happened</u> early Monday morning.

4 This poem <u>has read</u> by many people around the world.

C 주어진 문장을 수동태로 바꿔 쓰시오. (단, 「by+행위자」는 생략할 것)

1 Someone stole my bike last night.

→ _____ last night.

2 They will announce the winner at the end of the month.

→ _____ at the end of the month.

3 They have invited many people to the event.

→ _____ to the event.

4 They were making a big kite when I entered the classroom.

→ _____ when I entered the classroom.

30초 완성 map

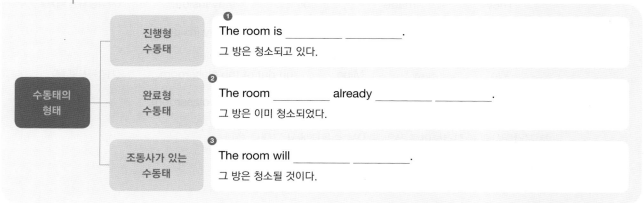

수동태의 형태	진행형 수동태	❶ The room is _____ _____. 그 방은 청소되고 있다.
	완료형 수동태	❷ The room _____ already _____ _____. 그 방은 이미 청소되었다.
	조동사가 있는 수동태	❸ The room will _____ _____. 그 방은 청소될 것이다.

4형식·5형식 문장의 수동태

1 4형식 문장의 수동태

4형식 문장은 간접목적어와 직접목적어를 각각 주어로 하여 두 개의 수동태를 만들 수 있다.

Sue	gave	him	two books.
		간접목적어	직접목적어

↓

He	**was given**	two books	by Sue.	〈간접목적어가 주어〉
Two books	**were given**	to him	by Sue.	〈직접목적어가 주어〉

↘ 직접목적어를 주어로 쓸 때는 간접목적어 앞에 알맞은 전치사를 써야 한다.

▶ buy, make, cook, write, get 등의 동사는 직접목적어를
주어로 하는 수동태만 쓸 수 있다.

Mia made the children gimbap.
→ Gimbap **was made** for the children by Mia. (○)
→ The children were made gimbap by Mia. (×)

> **간접목적어 앞에 쓰는 전치사**
> • to: send, bring, give, teach, tell 등
> • for: buy, make, cook, get 등

2 5형식 문장의 수동태

(1) 목적격보어가 명사, 형용사, to부정사, 분사일 때: 목적격보어의 형태가 변하지 않는다.

Many people	considered	Jane	a genius.	〈목적격보어: 명사〉
→ Jane	**was considered**		a genius.	

They	allowed	us	to enter the theater.	〈목적격보어: to부정사〉
→ We	**were allowed**		to enter the theater.	

We	saw	the boy	crossing the road.	〈목적격보어: 분사〉
→ The boy	**was seen**		crossing the road.	

(2) 목적격보어가 동사원형일 때: 동사원형을 to부정사로 바꾼다.

They	made	us	stay inside.	〈사역동사일 때〉
→ We	**were made**		**to stay** inside.	

We	saw	Mina	run out of the classroom.	〈지각동사일 때〉
→ Mina	**was seen**		**to run** out of the classroom.	

▶ 지각동사의 목적격보어로 쓰인 분사는 수동태에서 그대로 쓴다.

We saw Mina **running** out of the classroom.
→ Mina **was seen** *running* out of the classroom.

1 편지 한 통이 내게 보내졌다.
- ☐ A letter was sent to me.
- ☐ A letter was sent for me.

2 그는 멈추라는 말을 들었다.
- ☐ He told to stop.
- ☐ He was told to stop.

3 그가 노래하는 것이 들렸다.
- ☐ He was heard sing.
- ☐ He was heard to sing.

A 괄호 안에서 알맞은 것을 고르시오.

1 Many chances were given (to / for) us by our parents.

2 A huge meal was cooked (to / for) them to celebrate their victory.

3 The driver was made (to show / showing) his license by the police.

4 A tall man was seen (enter / entering) a house in our neighborhood.

5 John has been chosen (the leader / to the leader) of our team.

B 주어진 문장을 수동태로 바꿀 때, 빈칸에 알맞은 말을 쓰시오. (단, 「by+행위자」는 생략할 것)

1 They sent him lovely cards last year.
→ Lovely cards _____ last year.

2 They allowed us to play computer games on weekends.
→ We _____ computer games on weekends.

3 They saw David use his sister's smartphone.
→ David _____ his sister's smartphone.

C 밑줄 친 부분을 어법에 맞게 고쳐 쓰시오.

1 They were made <u>choose</u> between the two subjects.

2 The students will be taught <u>to English</u> next year.

3 He was advised <u>doing</u> exercise every day.

4 Lots of souvenirs were made <u>the visitors</u>.

30초 완성 map

수동태

4형식 문장
❶ Anna gave him several pens.
→ He _____ _____ several pens by Anna.
→ Several pens _____ _____ _____ him by Anna.

5형식 문장
❷ We call the dog Leo.
→ The dog _____ _____ _____ by us.
Mom made us clean the room.
→ We were made _____ _____ the room by Mom.

다양한 수동태

1 동사구의 수동태

여러 단어로 이루어진 동사구의 수동태는 동사를 「be동사+p.p.」로 바꾸고 나머지 부분은 그대로 써 준다.

My sister	looks after	the cats.
→ The cats	**are looked after**	by my sister.

hand in (제출하다)	→	**be handed in** (제출되다)
put off (미루다)	→	**be put off** (미뤄지다)
run over (치다)	→	**be run over** (치이다)
laugh at (비웃다)	→	**be laughed at** (비웃음을 당하다)
turn on/off (켜다/끄다)	→	**be turned on/off** (켜지다/꺼지다)
look up to (존경하다)	→	**be looked up to** (존경받다)
look down on (무시하다)	→	**be looked down on** (무시 당하다)
take care of (돌보다)	→	**be taken care of** (돌봐지다)

He **was laughed at** by everybody.
A rabbit **was run over** by a truck on the highway.
Ms. Jones **is looked up to** by her students.

주의 동사구의 목적어가 동사와 부사 사이에 있는 경우에는 수동태 문장에서 부사를 빠뜨리지 않도록 주의한다.
　　Justin **turned** the TV **off**.
　　→ The TV **was turned off** by Justin.

2 by 이외의 전치사를 쓰는 수동태

be filled with	~으로 가득 차다	**be covered** with	~으로 덮여 있다
be crowded with	~으로 붐비다	**be satisfied** with	~에 만족하다
be pleased with	~에 기뻐하다	**be disappointed** with〔at〕	~에 실망하다
be made up of	~으로 구성되다	**be surprised** at〔by〕	~에 놀라다
be interested in	~에 흥미가〔관심이〕 있다	**be tired** of	~에 싫증이 나다

The room **was filled** with balloons.
This band **is made up** of two girls and three boys.
I **am tired** of your endless complaints.
The store **was crowded** with young people.

시험 point

동사구의 수동태 형태

동사구의 수동태 문장에서 「by+목적격」이 이어지는 경우에는 동사구의 전치사나 부사, 또는 by를 빠뜨리지 않도록 주의한다.

Many dogs ┌ ☐ are taken care of ┐ Ms. Anderson.
　　　　　 └ ☐ are taken care of by ┘

1 TV가 켜졌다.
- ☐ The TV was turned.
- ☐ The TV was turned on.

2 그는 그들에게 비웃음을 당했다.
- ☐ He was laughed by them.
- ☐ He was laughed at by them.

3 그것은 물로 가득 차 있다.
- ☐ It is filled with water.
- ☐ It is filled by water.

A 괄호 안에서 알맞은 것을 고르시오.

1 I hope this song will be (listened / listened to) by many teens.

2 The missing painting is being looked (for / for by) the police.

3 The concert hall was crowded (by / with) fans from all over the world.

4 Jimmy is interested (in / by) reading books and watching movies.

5 Our baby brother will be looked after (us / by us) while our parents are out.

B 주어진 문장을 수동태로 바꿀 때, 빈칸에 알맞은 말을 쓰시오. (단, 「by+행위자」는 생략할 것)

1 We should hand in the reports by the end of this month.

→ The reports ＿＿＿＿＿＿＿＿＿＿＿＿＿ by the end of this month.

2 They will turn on the lights on the Christmas tree tomorrow.

→ The lights on the Christmas tree ＿＿＿＿＿＿＿＿＿＿＿ tomorrow.

3 People looked up to him because he saved many patients' lives.

→ He ＿＿＿＿＿＿＿＿＿＿＿ because he saved many patients' lives.

C 우리말과 일치하도록 괄호 안의 말을 이용하여 문장을 완성하시오.

1 대부분의 학생들이 그들의 성적에 기뻐했다. (please)

→ Most students ＿＿＿＿ ＿＿＿＿ ＿＿＿＿ their grades.

2 James가 집에 도착했을 때 그의 코트는 눈으로 덮여 있었다. (cover)

→ When James arrived home, his coat ＿＿＿＿ ＿＿＿＿ ＿＿＿＿ snow.

3 물은 수소와 산소 두 가지 기체로 구성된다. (make up)

→ Water ＿＿＿＿ ＿＿＿＿ ＿＿＿＿ ＿＿＿＿ two gases, hydrogen and oxygen.

30초 완성 map

다양한 수동태

동사구
❶ They look down on him because he is young.
→ He is ＿＿＿ ＿＿＿ ＿＿＿ by them because he is young.

by 이외의 전치사
❷ He was ＿＿＿ ＿＿＿ the results. 그는 결과에 만족했다.
I am ＿＿＿ ＿＿＿ this work. 나는 이 일에 싫증이 난다.

서술형 대비 문장 쓰기

Answers p. 14

↻ 문장 전환 주어진 문장을 수동태 문장으로 바꿔 쓰기

01 The police made him stop the car.

→ He _____ the car by the police.

02 They will show you the new machine next week.

→ The new machine _____ next week by them.

03 My mother is making a cake for my birthday.

→ A cake _____ for my birthday by my mother.

04 My grandma looked after me during summer vacation.

→ I _____ my grandma during summer vacation.

☐ 빈칸 완성 괄호 안의 말을 이용하여 빈칸 완성하기

05 나는 영어를 연습할 좋은 기회를 받았다. (give)

→ _____ a good opportunity to practice my English.

06 Jane은 아침 일찍 떠날 것을 조언 받았다. (advise, leave)

→ Jane _____ early in the morning.

07 그 배우들은 영화제에 초대받을 것이다. (will, invite)

→ The actors _____ to the film festival.

08 많은 팬들은 그 팀의 패배에 실망했다. (disappoint)

→ Many fans _____ the team's defeat.

✔ 오류 수정 어법에 맞게 문장 고쳐 쓰기

09 Tim was seen talk with a stranger near the park.

→ Tim _____ with a stranger near the park.

10 This bike was bought to my brother two years ago by my parents.

→ This bike _____ two years ago by my parents.

11 This grammar book is made up by 12 chapters.

→ This grammar book _____ 12 chapters.

12 The picnic will not put off even if it rains tomorrow.

→ The picnic _____ even if it rains tomorrow.

시험에 꼭 나오는 출제 포인트

Answers p. 14

출제 포인트 1 수동태로 쓸 수 없는 동사를 기억하자!

어법상 틀린 문장은?

① His wallet was stolen.
② English is spoken here.
③ My camera was disappeared.
④ Dinner will be prepared on time.
⑤ All of the questions must be answered.

출제 포인트 2 진행형과 완료형 수동태의 형태를 정확히 익혀 두자!

주어진 문장을 수동태로 바꿔 쓰시오.

(1) They are picking the cherries in the yard.
  → The cherries _____ _____
    _____ in the yard.
(2) My mom has written all these books.
  → All these books _____ _____
    _____ by my mom.

> **고득점 POINT** 조동사가 있는 문장의 수동태에서 조동사 다음에 be를 빠뜨리지 않도록 주의한다.
>
> **밑줄 친 부분을 어법에 맞게 고쳐 쓰시오.**
> The package must <u>delivered</u> before Friday.
> → _____

출제 포인트 3 사역동사와 지각동사의 수동태에서 동사원형은 to부정사로 바꾼다!

주어진 문장을 수동태로 바꿀 때, 빈칸에 알맞은 것은?

> Amy made Billy sing a song.
> → Billy was made _____ a song by Amy.

① sing   ② sang   ③ sung
④ singing   ⑤ to sing

> **고득점 POINT** 지각동사 수동태의 목적격보어 형태
>
> **빈칸에 알맞은 말을 모두 고르면?**
> She was seen _____ the room by him.
> ① enter   ② entered   ③ entering
> ④ to enter   ⑤ to entering

출제 포인트 4 동사구를 수동태로 쓸 때, by나 동사구의 일부를 빠뜨리지 않도록 주의하자!

다음 문장을 어법에 맞게 고쳐 다시 쓰시오.

> The baby will be taken care of her aunt.

→ The baby will _____.

실전 Test

[01-02] 다음 문장을 수동태로 바꿀 때, 빈칸에 알맞은 말을 고르시오. |4점, 각 2점|

01

Mia wrote the letter yesterday.
→ The letter _____ by Mia yesterday.

① written
② is wrote
③ is written
④ was write
⑤ was written

02

They have finished the work.
→ The work _____ by them.

① is finished
② was finished
③ has been finished
④ have been finished
⑤ was had finished

[03-04] 다음 빈칸에 들어갈 말로 알맞은 것을 고르시오. |4점, 각 2점|

03

The song will _____ by a famous rock star.

① sing
② be sing
③ be sung
④ have sung
⑤ be singing

04

The cupcakes _____ by my mom.

① have baked
② been baked
③ have been baking
④ have been baked
⑤ have being baked

05 우리말과 일치하도록 문장을 완성할 때, 빈칸에 들어갈 말로 알맞은 것은? |3점|

그 건물은 우리 회사에 의해 지어지고 있다.
→ The building _____ by our company.

① being built
② is been built
③ is being built
④ is been building
⑤ has being built

06 빈칸에 들어갈 말이 나머지와 다른 것은? |3점|

① He was pleased _____ the results.
② Amy must be tired _____ waiting for him.
③ The bus was very crowded _____ students this morning.
④ My heart was filled _____ pride at that time.
⑤ The travelers are satisfied _____ the local food.

07 주어진 문장을 수동태로 바꿀 때, 다섯 번째로 오는 단어는? |4점|

My family named the dog Pinky.

① family
② was
③ dog
④ Pinky
⑤ named

08 밑줄 친 부분 중 어법상 옳은 것은? |4점|

① The wolf <u>was appeared</u> suddenly.
② The building <u>is had</u> by a famous actor.
③ The chicken <u>will be cooked</u> in 30 minutes.
④ The picture <u>took</u> by a young photographer.
⑤ Mr. Jackson <u>is resembled</u> by his daughter.

09 주어진 문장을 수동태로 바르게 바꾼 것을 <u>모두</u> 고르면? |4점|

> I gave him a cup of tea.

① He was given a cup of tea to me.
② He was given a cup of tea by me.
③ A cup of tea was given him by me.
④ A cup of tea was given to him by me.
⑤ A cup of tea was given to me by him.

최신기출

12 다음 문장을 주어진 단어로 시작하는 문장으로 바꿀 때, 쓰이지 <u>않는</u> 단어는? |4점|

> My teacher bought us ice cream.
> → Ice cream _____.

① by   ② us   ③ to
④ was   ⑤ bought

10 밑줄 친 부분이 어법상 <u>틀린</u> 것끼리 짝지어진 것은? |4점|

> ⓐ The robbers <u>will be caught</u> soon.
> ⓑ The project <u>can't been finished</u> that fast.
> ⓒ The sweater <u>should be washing</u> by hand.
> ⓓ The match <u>will be canceled</u> if it rains.
> ⓔ The news <u>can be delivered</u> faster than you think.

① ⓐ, ⓓ   ② ⓐ, ⓔ   ③ ⓑ, ⓒ
④ ⓑ, ⓔ   ⑤ ⓒ, ⓓ

13 빈칸에 들어갈 말이 같은 것끼리 짝지어진 것은? |4점|

> ⓐ We were surprised _____ his return.
> ⓑ Each team is made up _____ five players.
> ⓒ I was disappointed _____ my math scores.
> ⓓ He is tired _____ staying in the library all day.

① ⓐ, ⓑ – ⓒ, ⓓ   ② ⓐ, ⓒ – ⓑ, ⓓ
③ ⓐ, ⓓ – ⓑ, ⓒ   ④ ⓐ – ⓑ, ⓒ, ⓓ
⑤ ⓐ, ⓒ, ⓓ – ⓑ

11 주어진 문장을 수동태로 <u>잘못</u> 바꾼 것은? |4점|

① A stranger was following me.
   → I was being followed by a stranger.
② He should carry those boxes.
   → Those boxes should be carried by him.
③ James have owned this house for a year.
   → This house has been owned by James for a year.
④ They are painting the house now.
   → The house is painting by them now.
⑤ She has just finished her homework.
   → Her homework has just been finished by her.

고난도

14 어법상 <u>틀린</u> 문장의 개수는? |5점|

> ⓐ The present was sent for me by my uncle.
> ⓑ This toy car was made for me by my dad.
> ⓒ The two players were seen fight.
> ⓓ She was made to angry by her son's rude behavior.

① 없음   ② 1개   ③ 2개   ④ 3개   ⑤ 4개

15 빈칸에 알맞은 말이 순서대로 바르게 짝지어진 것은? |4점|

- We were made _____ some articles.
- The woman was heard _____ loudly by her neighbors.

*article 기사

① read – shout
② read – to shout
③ read – shouting
④ to read – shout
⑤ to read – to shout

16 밑줄 친 부분을 잘못 고친 것은? |5점|

ⓐ The T-shirt was cost over $100.
ⓑ A big dog was appeared in front of me.
ⓒ The cat and dog are taken care of Greg.
ⓓ Mike was laughed by his classmates.
ⓔ The light is always turning on and off by him.

① ⓐ → was cost by
② ⓑ → appeared
③ ⓒ → taken care of by
④ ⓓ → laughed at
⑤ ⓔ → turned

17 다음 글의 밑줄 친 ①~⑤ 중 어법상 틀린 것은? |4점|

My family went hiking last Sunday. The road ① was covered with red and yellow leaves. The mountain ② was crowded with hikers, but we ③ were pleased with the beautiful scenery. My mom ④ is interested with photography, so she took a lot of pictures. She ⑤ was satisfied with the pictures. It was a great day!

*scenery 풍경

서술형

18 우리말과 일치하도록 괄호 안의 말을 이용하여 빈칸에 알맞은 말을 쓰시오. |6점, 각 2점|

(1) 이 웹사이트는 많은 학생들에 의해 방문된다. (visit)

→ This website _____ _____ by many students.

(2) 어젯밤에 TV가 언제 꺼졌니? (turn off)

→ When _____ the TV _____ _____ last night?

(3) 이 식당은 오랫동안 문이 닫혀있다. (close)

→ This restaurant _____ _____ _____ for a long time.

[19-20] 다음 문장을 수동태로 바꿔 쓸 때, 빈칸에 알맞은 말을 쓰시오. |6점, 각 3점|

19

You must hand in the report on time.

→ The report _____ on time.

20

We heard the baby crying in the room.

→ The baby _____ in the room.

21 우리말과 일치하도록 괄호 안의 말을 바르게 배열하시오. |3점|

그 지붕은 다음 달에 노란색으로 칠해질 것이다.
(yellow, will, painted, next month, be, the roof)

→ _____

개념 우선 확인 | 밑줄 친 접속사의 의미 고르기

1 <u>As</u> John won the game, he was happy.

☐ ~하면서 ☐ ~이기 때문에

2 <u>Since</u> I moved here, I have made many friends.

☐ ~ 이후로 ☐ ~이기 때문에

3 They sat in the front <u>so that</u> they could hear well.

☐ 그래서 ☐ ~하기 위해서

A 괄호 안에서 알맞은 것을 고르시오.

1 (As / Until) I arrived at the town, it started to snow.

2 We will have to wait until they (come / will come) to us.

3 Nobody has seen Suji (when / since) she left school early yesterday.

4 The thief started to run (while / as soon as) he saw a police officer.

5 The accident happened (because / because of) both drivers were driving too fast.

B 빈칸에 알맞은 접속사를 〈보기〉에서 골라 쓰시오. (단, 한 번씩만 쓸 것)

보기	since	while	so that

1 Fasten your seat belt _____ you are driving.

2 Our lives have changed a lot _____ Edison invented the light bulb.

3 My mother will come to my school _____ she can speak with my teacher.

C 우리말과 일치하도록 괄호 안의 말을 바르게 배열하여 문장을 완성하시오.

1 너는 네 이름이 불릴 때까지 밖에서 기다려야 한다. (your, is, until, name, called)

→ You should wait outside _____.

2 나는 지갑을 집에 두고 와서 인호에게 돈을 좀 빌려야 했다. (left, at, my wallet, since, home, I)

→ _____, I had to borrow some money from Inho.

3 감기에 걸리지 않기 위해서 손을 자주 씻어야 한다. (you, so, a cold, catch, don't, that)

→ You should wash your hands often _____.

30초 완성 map

부사절 접속사

시간

❶ The bus left _____ _____ _____ I got there.
내가 그곳에 도착하자마자 버스는 떠났다.
When he _____, we will start the game.
그가 도착할 때 우리는 경기를 시작할 것이다.

이유

❷ He can't come (since / while) he is busy. 그는 바빠서 올 수 없다.

목적

❸ We practiced hard _____ _____ we could win the contest.
우리는 대회에서 우승하기 위해서 열심히 연습했다.

조건·양보의 접속사, 명사절을 이끄는 접속사

1 조건의 접속사

if	(만약) ~하면	**If** you exercise every day, you will be healthy.
unless	(만약) ~하지 않으면 (= if ~ not)	**Unless** we leave now, we will miss the train. (= **If** we **don't** leave now, we will miss the train.)

> 조건의 부사절에서는 미래를 나타낼 때 현재시제를 쓴다.
>
> If it **rains** tomorrow, we will stay home.
> └ will rain (×)

주의 unless는 부정의 의미를 포함하고 있으므로 not과 함께 쓰지 않도록 주의한다.
He will come to the party unless he **is** busy.
└ isn't (×)

2 양보의 접속사

although though even though	~에도 불구하고, 비록 ~이지만	**Although** it was his fault, he didn't say sorry. He still looks hungry **even though** he ate a whole pizza.

> 같은 의미의 전치사(구)인 despite나 in spite of 다음에는 명사(구)가 온다.
>
> **Despite〔In spite of〕** *his illness*, he didn't lose hope.
> = **Though〔Although〕** he was ill, he didn't lose hope.

3 명사절을 이끄는 접속사 if/whether

if whether	~인지 (아닌지)	I wonder **if〔whether〕** she likes flowers.

> if가 이끄는 명사절은 문장에서 목적어로만 쓰일 수 있지만, whether가 이끄는 명사절은 문장에서 주어,
> 목적어, 보어로 쓰일 수 있다.
>
> **Whether** he will come is not certain. 〈주어〉
> └ If (×)

비교 point

조건의 접속사 if vs. 명사절을 이끄는 접속사 if

미래시제를 나타낼 때, if 조건절에서는 현재시제를 쓰지만 if 명사절에서는 미래시제를 쓴다.

1 I want to know if it (rains / will rain) tomorrow.   나는 내일 비가 올지 알고 싶다.

2 The game will be canceled if it (rains / will rain) tomorrow.   내일 비가 온다면 그 경기는 취소될 것이다.

개념 우선 확인 | 밑줄 친 부분의 의미 고르기

1 I won't go <u>unless you come</u>.
- ☐ 네가 온다면
- ☐ 네가 오지 않으면

2 <u>Though it was raining</u>, we went out.
- ☐ 비가 오고 있었지만
- ☐ 비가 오고 있어서

3 I wonder <u>if he knows my name</u>.
- ☐ 그가 내 이름을 안다면
- ☐ 그가 내 이름을 아는지

A 괄호 안에서 알맞은 것을 고르시오.

1 You can't buy alcohol (if / unless) you are over 18. *alcohol 술, 주류

2 He couldn't pass the exam (if / even though) he studied hard.

3 I can't decide (though / whether) I want to attend the meeting.

4 (If / Unless) you don't use your smartphone before bed, you will sleep well.

5 If you (get / will get) home late, your parents will be angry.

B 빈칸에 알맞은 접속사를 〈보기〉에서 골라 쓰시오.

보기	if	unless	although

1 We will not begin _____ everyone is ready.

2 I don't know _____ the rumor is true or not.

3 _____ the play was boring, the actors were great.

C 어법상 <u>틀린</u> 부분을 찾아 바르게 고쳐 쓰시오. (단, 한 곳만 고쳐 쓸 것)

1 Unless you don't get up now, you'll be late for school.

2 Despite he didn't have much time, he came to see us.

3 I wonder if Tom went camping tomorrow.

4 If they will come early, I will make some sandwiches for them.

5 The most important thing is if you like my present or not.

30초 완성 map

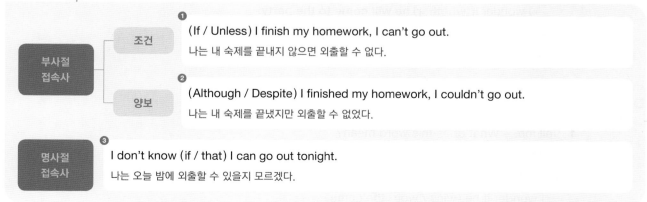

부사절 접속사
- 조건 — ❶ (If / Unless) I finish my homework, I can't go out.
  나는 내 숙제를 끝내지 않으면 외출할 수 없다.
- 양보 — ❷ (Although / Despite) I finished my homework, I couldn't go out.
  나는 내 숙제를 끝냈지만 외출할 수 없었다.

명사절 접속사
- ❸ I don't know (if / that) I can go out tonight.
  나는 오늘 밤에 외출할 수 있을지 모르겠다.

1 상관접속사

상관접속사는 두 단어가 짝을 이루어 단어와 단어, 구와 구, 또는 절과 절을 연결하는 것을 말한다.

both A and B	A와 B 둘 다	**Both** my brother **and** I are at home now.
either A or B	A나 B 둘 중 하나	She majored in **either** biology **or** physics.
neither A nor B	A도 B도 아닌	This movie is **neither** interesting **nor** scary.
not only A but (also) B = B as well as A	A뿐만 아니라 B도	Joe is **not only** kind **but also** polite. = Joe is polite **as well as** kind.

▶ both A and B가 주어로 쓰인 경우에는 항상 복수 취급하고, 나머지는 B의 인칭과 수에 동사를 일치시킨다.

Neither his parents **nor** *Eric* was born in Austria.

Amy, **as well as** her sisters, likes cats.

2 간접의문문

의문문이 어떤 문장의 일부가 되어 주어, 목적어, 보어로 쓰이는 경우, 이 문장을 간접의문문이라고 한다.

(1) 의문사가 있는 경우: 「의문사＋주어＋동사」

> I don't know. + What is he doing?
> → I don't know **what he is doing**.

▶ 주절의 동사가 think, believe, guess 등인 의문문의 경우에는 간접의문문의 의문사를 문장의 맨 앞에 쓴다.

Do you think? + **Why** is Bob wearing funny clothes?

→ **Why** do you think **Bob is wearing funny clothes**?

주의 의문사가 주어일 경우에는 「의문사(주어)＋동사」의 어순으로 쓴다.

Tell me. + Who made the cookies? → Tell me **who made** the cookies.

(2) 의문사가 없는 경우: 「if〔whether〕＋주어＋동사」

> I wonder. + Will he come to the party?
> → I wonder **if〔whether〕 he will come to the party**.

시험 point

간접의문문의 시제와 수 일치

의문문을 간접의문문으로 바꿀 때 동사의 시제와 수 일치에 주의한다.

1 Tell me. + What does this word mean?

→ Tell me what this word (mean / means).

2 I wonder. + Did he win the game?

→ I wonder if he (wins / won) the game.

개념 우선 확인 | 옳은 표현 고르기

1 A나 B 둘 중 하나를 선택하다
- ☐ choose either *A* or *B*
- ☐ choose both *A* and *B*

2 A뿐만 아니라 B도 좋아하다
- ☐ like neither *A* nor *B*
- ☐ like not only *A* but also *B*

3 그의 이름이 무엇인지 모르다
- ☐ don't know what is his name
- ☐ don't know what his name is

A 괄호 안에서 알맞은 것을 고르시오.

1 He can speak (neither / both) Chinese nor Japanese.

2 Rick will call us (either / both) tonight or tomorrow night.

3 I want to visit (either / both) Paris and London when I go to Europe.

4 They like not only going to new places (and also / but also) meeting new people.

B 밑줄 친 부분을 어법에 맞게 고쳐 쓰시오.

1 Can you tell me where can I get more information about this?

2 I feel like neither going shopping or going to the movies.

3 Both Suji and Inho is going to help us organize the event.

4 Not only you but also Peter are going to learn Japanese.

C 우리말과 일치하도록 괄호 안의 말을 바르게 배열하여 문장을 완성하시오.

1 엄마는 커피도 차도 좋아하지 않으신다. (likes, coffee, neither, tea, nor)

→ Mom _____ .

2 나는 Tom이 그 파티에 갔었는지 궁금하다. (Tom, to, went, the party, whether)

→ I wonder _____ .

3 집에 오는 길에 낯선 사람이 내게 지하철역이 어디에 있는지 물었다.
(was, asked, where, me, the subway station)

→ On my way home, a stranger _____ .

4 너는 왜 Jane이 화가 났었다고 생각하니? (why, you, do, Jane, think, angry, was)

→ _____ ?

30초 완성 map

상관접속사
Both Jane and Tom (is / are) coming.
He likes _____ _____ hamburgers _____ _____ hot dogs.
그는 햄버거뿐만 아니라 핫도그도 좋아한다.

간접의문문
I don't know where (Jane was / was Jane).
I don't know _____ he wanted to go. 나는 그가 가기를 원했는지 모른다.

서술형 대비 문장 쓰기

Answers p. 16

□ 빈칸 완성 괄호 안의 말을 이용하여 빈칸 완성하기

01 그녀는 제주도에 도착하자마자 내게 문자메시지를 보냈다. (as soon as, arrive)

→ _____ at Jeju-do, she sent me a text message.

02 네가 콘서트에 늦으면 네 친구들은 매우 화가 날 것이다. (if, be, late)

→ _____ for the concert, your friends will be very angry.

03 민수는 더 잘 집중하기 위해서 이어폰을 끼고 공부를 한다. (so that, can, concentrate)

→ Minsu studies with earphones on _____ better.

04 Emily도 그녀의 부모님도 프랑스어를 하지 못한다. (neither, Emily, her parents, speak)

→ _____ French.

✔ 오류 수정 어법에 맞게 문장 고쳐 쓰기

05 He will come and help us unless he isn't too busy.

→ He will come and help us _____.

06 They wanted to know how did I solve the math problem.

→ They wanted to know _____.

07 Both Jane and Tom is in our study group.

→ _____ in our study group.

08 I usually spend my weekends either watching TV or play games.

→ I usually spend my weekends _____.

☰ 배열 영작 괄호 안의 말을 바르게 배열하기

09 나는 그가 내 이름을 기억하는지 궁금하다. (wonder, remembers, if, he, I)

→ _____ my name.

10 비록 그는 숙제가 많았지만 친구들을 만나러 나갔다. (although, had, homework, a lot of, he)

→ _____, he went out to meet his friends.

11 Mike는 재능이 있을 뿐만 아니라 열심히 노력한다. (hardworking, but also, not only, talented)

→ Mike is _____.

12 그는 일찍 일어나기 위해 일찍 잠자리에 들었다. (so, he, early, get up, that, could)

→ He went to bed early _____.

시험에 꼭 나오는 출제 포인트

Answers p. 16

출제 포인트 1 시간이나 조건의 부사절에서는 미래의 일을 현재시제로 나타낸다!

각 빈칸에 come을 알맞은 형태로 바꿔 쓰시오.

(1) We will start the party when my father _____ home.

　　(우리는 아버지가 집에 오실 때 파티를 시작할 것이다.)

(2) I want to know if my father _____ back next week.

　　(나는 아버지가 다음 주에 돌아오실지 알고 싶다.)

출제 포인트 2 접속사 다음에는 절이 오고, 전치사 다음에는 명사(구)가 온다!

괄호 안에서 알맞은 것을 고르시오.

The machine was covered with dust (because / because of) it had not been used for years.

> **고득점 POINT** 전치사 despite는 뒤에 명사(구)가 온다.
>
> **괄호 안에서 알맞은 것을 고르시오.**
>
> (Although / Despite) all her efforts, she didn't win the race.

출제 포인트 3 상관접속사의 형태에 주의하자!

어법상 틀린 부분을 찾아 바르게 고쳐 쓰시오.

(1) Emma can speak not only English and also French.

(2) I either go swimming or riding my bike every day.

> **고득점 POINT** 상관접속사 주어의 동사 수 일치
>
> **빈칸에 like를 알맞은 형태로 쓰시오. (단, 현재형으로 쓸 것)**
>
> (1) Neither you nor Ben _____ Chinese food.
>
> (2) Both you and Ben _____ Italian food.

출제 포인트 4 의문문을 간접의문문으로 쓸 때, 어순에 주의하자!

두 문장을 한 문장으로 연결하여 쓰시오.

(1) I wonder. + How did you get here?

　　→ I wonder _____.

(2) I want to know. + Do you like skiing?

　　→ I want to know _____.

> **고득점 POINT** think, believe, guess 등의 동사가 쓰이면 간접의문문의 의문사를 문장 맨 앞에 써야 한다.
>
> **두 문장을 한 문장으로 연결하시오.**
>
> Do you think? + Where did she go last night?
>
> → _____ last night?

유형	문항수	배점	점수
객관식	17	60	
서술형	10	40	

[01-03] 다음 빈칸에 들어갈 말로 가장 알맞은 것을 고르시오.
|6점, 각 2점|

01

He read a book _____ he was waiting for the bus.

① if　　　　② that　　　　③ while

④ so　　　　⑤ though

02

_____ he was really tired, he went to bed immediately.

① As　　　　② Until　　　　③ While

④ After　　　⑤ Though

03

_____ I tried my best, I couldn't change her mind.

① If　　　　② Because　　　③ While

④ Since　　　⑤ Though

04 빈칸에 알맞은 get의 형태가 순서대로 바르게 짝지어진 것은? |4점|

• I will see a doctor if the symptoms _____ worse.

• I wonder if she _____ up early tomorrow.

① get – gets　　　　② get – will get

③ will get – gets　　④ will get – will get

⑤ are getting – gets

05 다음 두 문장을 한 문장으로 나타낼 때, 빈칸에 들어갈 말로 알맞은 것은? |3점|

Please tell me. + How old is this building?
→ Please tell me _____.

① how is old this building

② this building how old is

③ how this building is old

④ how old is this building

⑤ how old this building is

06 빈칸에 공통으로 들어갈 말로 알맞은 것은? |3점|

• Do you know _____ they will go to the movies tonight?

• _____ you enjoy the work or not is important.

① if〔If〕　　　　　　② as〔As〕

③ while〔While〕　　　④ though〔Though〕

⑤ whether〔Whether〕

07 (A)~(C)에 들어갈 말이 바르게 짝지어진 것은? |4점|

• You should check the bus schedule (A) before / since you leave.

• We went swimming (B) though / since it was so hot.

• I am saving money (C) so that / because I can buy a new smartphone.

	(A)	(B)	(C)
①	before	····· though	····· so that
②	before	····· since	····· so that
③	before	····· though	····· because
④	since	····· since	····· because
⑤	since	····· though	····· so that

[08-09] 두 문장의 의미가 같도록 할 때, 빈칸에 들어갈 말로 알맞은 것을 고르시오. |6점, 각 3점|

08

> You will fail the test if you don't study hard.
> = You will fail the test _____ you study hard.

① as   ② though   ③ unless

④ despite   ⑤ whether

09

> We stood up in order to see the game better.
> = We stood up _____ we could see the game better.

① that

② so as

③ so that

④ so as to

⑤ such that

고난도

10 밑줄 친 부분이 어법상 틀린 문장의 개수는? |5점|

> ⓐ Either you or Ken <u>have</u> to stay here.
> ⓑ Not only Tina but also her sister <u>has</u> a cold.
> ⓒ Steve, as well as his friends, <u>was</u> surprised at the news.
> ⓓ Neither Ann nor I <u>have</u> to come here.
> ⓔ Both Mike and his brother <u>speaks</u> Spanish fluently.

① 1개   ② 2개   ③ 3개   ④ 4개   ⑤ 5개

11 어법상 틀린 문장은? |4점|

① Do you know who ate my cake?

② Do you think why he came back?

③ Please wait for me until I finish my homework.

④ He not only sings well but also dances well.

⑤ We couldn't go out because of the bad weather.

12 밑줄 친 부분과 바꿔 쓸 수 없는 것은? |4점|

① <u>Since</u> I felt tired, I went to bed earlier.
    (→ Because)

② <u>As</u> we were having dinner, Mike arrived.
    (→ While)

③ <u>Though</u> he is young, he is very wise.
    (→ Although)

④ We will play basketball <u>if</u> we have free time.
                 (→ whether)

⑤ <u>Despite</u> our worries, the event went well.
    (→ In spite of)

13 우리말과 일치하도록 할 때, 빈칸에 들어갈 말로 알맞은 것은? |4점|

> 누가 그 창문을 깼는지 아무도 모른다.
> → Nobody knows _____.

① who broke the window

② who breaks the window

③ who didn't break the window

④ did who break the window

⑤ broke who the window

고난도

14 밑줄 친 접속사의 의미가 서로 같은 것끼리 짝지어진 것은? |5점|

① It will be fun <u>if</u> he joins us.
    I don't know <u>if</u> she will come to school.

② I lived in New York <u>when</u> I was little.
    My family was sleeping <u>when</u> I got home.

③ You may drive slowly <u>since</u> we have time.
    His uncle has taken care of him <u>since</u> he was a little kid.

④ <u>As</u> Mike is kind, everyone loves him.
    <u>As</u> I got off the bus, I saw my dad.

⑤ Lily did laundry <u>while</u> her baby was sleeping.
    <u>While</u> Sam loves sports, Joe loves reading.

15 어법상 옳은 것끼리 짝지어진 것은? |5점|

ⓐ Despite this bike is small, he can ride it.

ⓑ If you will take an umbrella, you won't get wet in the rain.

ⓒ Minsu didn't answer the phone since he was very busy.

ⓓ Unless the weather isn't nice, we won't go out.

ⓔ While I prefer being alone, my sister prefers being with people.

① ⓐ, ⓒ ② ⓒ, ⓔ ③ ⓐ, ⓒ, ⓔ
④ ⓑ, ⓒ, ⓓ ⑤ ⓐ, ⓒ, ⓓ, ⓔ

[16-17] 다음 글을 읽고, 물음에 답하시오.

When we need a new word, we can ___(A)___ create one or borrow one from another language. For example, we created words like "popcorn" by combining two words. "Tomato" was borrowed from Spanish. (B) 우리는 심지어 제품뿐만 아니라 사람의 이름도 차용한다. "Sandwich" was named after the Earl of Sandwich.

*combine 결합시키다 Earl 백작

16 빈칸 (A)에 들어갈 말로 알맞은 것은? |3점|

① both ② either ③ all
④ neither ⑤ not only

17 밑줄 친 (B)를 영어로 옮길 때, 빈칸에 알맞은 것을 모두 고르면? |4점|

We even borrow names from _____.

① both products and people
② either products or people
③ neither products nor people
④ not only products but also people
⑤ people as well as products

서술형

18 빈칸에 알맞은 접속사를 〈보기〉에서 골라 쓰시오. (단, 한 번씩만 사용할 것) |6점, 각 2점|

보기   while   since   as soon as

(1) _____ he has visited Rome many times, he knows the city well.

(2) I like carrots very much, _____ my sister never eats them.

(3) _____ the child saw his mother, he stopped crying.

[19-20] 주어진 문장과 의미가 같도록 빈칸에 알맞은 말을 쓰시오. |4점, 각 2점|

19 He can speak Chinese as well as Spanish.

→ He can speak _____ _____ Spanish _____ _____ Chinese.

20 Steve turned on the light in order to read a book.

→ Steve turned on the light _____ _____ he could read a book.

개념 우선 확인 | 옳은 해석 고르기

1 the student who likes you
- ☐ 너를 좋아하는 학생
- ☐ 네가 좋아하는 학생

2 a student whose major is math
- ☐ 전공이 수학인 학생
- ☐ 누구의 전공이 수학인지

3 What he studies is math.
- ☐ 무엇을 공부하는가는 수학이다.
- ☐ 그가 공부하는 것은 수학이다.

A 괄호 안에서 알맞은 것을 고르시오.

1 My father bought me (what / that) I wanted.

2 I have a friend (who / whose) parents are both scientists.

3 These are the boys (whom / whose) Emily met at the party.

4 We will visit a town (that / what) is famous for its old streets.

B 〈보기〉에서 알맞은 관계대명사를 골라 두 문장을 한 문장으로 연결하시오. (단, 한 번씩만 사용할 것)

보기	who	whose	what	that

1 I heard the song. Jane wrote the song.

→ I heard _____ Jane wrote.

2 We helped the boy. The boy's dog was missing.

→ We helped _____ dog was missing.

3 He met the girl. The girl won the school speech contest.

→ He met _____ won the school speech contest.

4 I don't know the thing. You are looking for the thing.

→ I don't know _____ you are looking for.

C 밑줄 친 부분을 어법에 맞게 고쳐 쓰시오.

1 A good friend is <u>which</u> you need.

2 The children whom you met last Sunday <u>was</u> from Spain.

3 Tom showed me the pictures <u>what</u> he took during his trip.

30초 완성 map

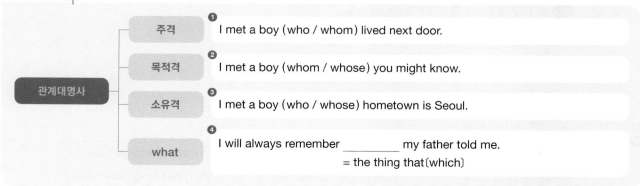

관계대명사

주격 ❶ I met a boy (who / whom) lived next door.

목적격 ❷ I met a boy (whom / whose) you might know.

소유격 ❸ I met a boy (who / whose) hometown is Seoul.

what ❹ I will always remember _____ my father told me.
= the thing that(which)

주의해야 할 관계대명사의 쓰임

1 「주격 관계대명사 + be동사」의 생략

「주격 관계대명사 + be동사」 다음에 현재분사나 과거분사가 오는 경우, 「주격 관계대명사 + be동사」를 생략할 수 있다.

> She saw a man **who(that) was** wearing a brown suit.
>
> → She saw a man wearing a brown suit.

I read the story **which was** written by my grandmother.
→ I read the story written by my grandmother.

2 전치사 + 관계대명사

관계대명사가 전치사의 목적어로 쓰인 경우, 전치사는 관계대명사절 끝에 오거나 관계대명사 앞에 올 수 있다.

This is the man	**who(m)(that)**	we were talking **about**.
→ This is the man	**about whom**	we were talking.

▶ 전치사가 관계대명사 앞에 쓰인 경우에는 관계대명사를 생략할 수 없다.

I will visit the city in which he lived. = I will visit the city (which) he lived in.
└─ 생략 불가

주의 관계대명사 who나 that 앞에는 전치사가 올 수 없으며, 이때는 전치사가 관계사절 끝에 와야 한다.
She likes the people **with whom** she is working.
└─ who(that) (×)

3 관계대명사의 계속적 용법

선행사에 대해 추가 설명을 할 때 쓰며, 관계사 앞에 콤마(,)를 쓴다.

This book is about King Sejong,	**who** invented Hangul. = and he	이 책은 세종대왕에 관한 것인데, 그는 한글을 발명했다.

The watch,	**which** I bought yesterday,	was very expensive.	그 시계는 어제 내가 산 것인데, 매우 비쌌다.

▶ 계속적 용법의 관계대명사 which는 앞 문장 전체를 선행사로 취할 수 있다.

He didn't come, **which** disappointed me. 그가 오지 않았는데, 그것이 나를 실망시켰다.
└─선행사   = and it

주의 관계대명사 that은 계속적 용법으로 쓸 수 없다.
We ate kimchi, **which** is a traditional Korean food.
└─ that (×)

시험 point
관계대명사 that을 쓸 수 없는 경우

「전치사 + 관계대명사」로 쓸 때	Do you know the boy with (whom / that) Kevin is talking?
계속적 용법으로 쓸 때	Do you remember Mina, (who / that) has long brown hair?

1 내가 살았던 도시
- ☐ the city which I lived
- ☐ the city in which I lived

2 그곳에 서 있는 남자
- ☐ the man standing there
- ☐ the man who standing there

3 Tim은 배우인데, 키가 크다.
- ☐ Tim who is an actor is tall.
- ☐ Tim, who is an actor, is tall.

A 괄호 안에서 알맞은 것을 고르시오.

1 Mom found the doll (for which / which for) I was looking.

2 We have a plan to visit the city, (that / which) makes us excited.

3 I am reading the novel on (that / which) the movie is based.

4 The woman (is sitting / sitting) on the bench is my aunt.

5 This is the man about (who / whom) I wrote in my letter.

B 다음 문장에서 생략할 수 있는 부분을 찾아 괄호로 표시하시오. (없으면 × 표시할 것)

1 The girls whom you talked about are waiting for you now.

2 She bought a book which was written in easy English.

3 What is the name of the hotel that you stayed at last month?

4 The man with whom I went shopping yesterday is my father.

C 우리말과 일치하도록 빈칸에 알맞은 관계대명사를 쓰시오.

1 그는 약속을 어겼는데, 그것은 큰 실수였다.

→ He broke his promise, _____ was a big mistake.

2 나는 그가 사랑에 빠진 여자를 안다.

→ I know the woman with _____ he fell in love.

3 그녀는 나에게 그녀의 남동생의 사진을 보여주었는데, 그는 유명한 피아니스트이다.

→ She showed me a picture of her brother, _____ is a famous pianist.

30초 완성 map

관계대명사

생략

❶ Do you know the girl **who is** wearing a hat?
→ Do you know the girl _____ _____ _____ ?

전치사 + 관계대명사

❷ This is the house **that** he was born **in**.
= This is the house _____ _____ he was born.

계속적 용법

❸ Mia, (who / that) is my best friend, lives in London.
I said nothing, (which / that) made her angry.

unit 3 관계부사

1 관계부사의 쓰임

관계부사는 시간, 장소, 이유, 방법을 나타내는 선행사를 수식하는 절을 이끌며 문장에서 「접속사＋부사(구)」의 역할을 한다.

I remember the place.		＋	We first met in the place.
→ I remember the place	**where**		we first met.

2 관계부사의 종류

선행사	관계부사	
장소 (the place, the city 등)	**where**	He forgot the place **where** he parked his car. This is the bakery **where** I buy bread every Sunday.
시간 (the time, the day 등)	**when**	Tomorrow is the day **when** the vacation starts. I remember the time **when** the accident happened.
이유 (the reason)	**why**	I don't know the reason **why** she was late. That is the reason **why** he got angry.
방법 (the way)	**how**	I want to know **how** you solved the problem. = I want to know the way you solved the problem.

주의 관계부사 how와 선행사 the way는 함께 쓸 수 없다.

▶ 선행사가 the place, the time, the reason일 때는 선행사나 관계부사 중 하나를 생략할 수 있다.

I don't remember **the place where** I put my key.
= I don't remember **the place** I put my key. / I don't remember **where** I put my key.

3 관계부사를 「전치사＋관계대명사」로 나타내기

where	at/on/in which	This is the drawer **where** I keep my passport. = This is the drawer **in which** I keep my passport.
when	at/on/in which	I will never forget the day **when** I won the Olympic medal. = I will never forget the day **on which** I won the Olympic medal.
why	for which	I don't know the reason **why** you like him. = I don't know the reason **for which** you like him.

비교 point 관계대명사 vs. 관계부사

관계대명사와 관계부사 중 무엇을 쓸지는 선행사가 관계사절에서 하는 역할로 구분한다.

1 London is the city (which / where) I visited last year. ← I visited **the city** last year. 〈목적어: 명사〉

2 London is the city (which / where) I met Tom last year. ← I met Tom **in the city** last year. 〈부사구〉

개념 우선 확인 | 옳은 표현 고르기

1 그가 사는 집
- ☐ the house which he lives
- ☐ the house where he lives

2 그가 태어난 날
- ☐ the day when he was born
- ☐ the day where he was born

3 그가 떠난 이유
- ☐ the reason how he left
- ☐ the reason why he left

A 괄호 안에서 알맞은 것을 고르시오.

1 Seoul is a city (that / where) many people live.

2 Do you know the reason (how / why) Jane decided not to come to the party?

3 Today is the day (where / when) we start the new school year.

4 This is the (way / how) he discovered the hidden treasure on the island.

B 두 문장을 관계부사를 이용하여 한 문장으로 연결하시오.

1 We want to know the reason. You are always late for that reason.
→ We want to know _____.

2 Jim showed me the way. He fixed his smartphone in that way.
→ Jim showed me _____.

3 We visited the town. The famous poet was born in that town.
→ We visited _____.

4 I still remember the day. We bought our first car on that day.
→ I still remember _____.

C 밑줄 친 부분을 어법에 맞게 고쳐 쓰시오.

1 I'm looking for a place <u>which</u> I can ride a bike.

2 Tim will tell you <u>the way how</u> you can join the club.

3 Tomorrow is the day <u>on when</u> we go to see our favorite singer.

30초 완성 map

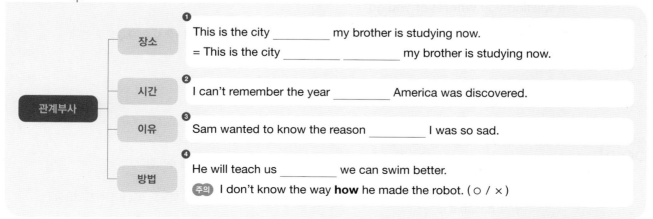

장소
❶ This is the city _____ my brother is studying now.
= This is the city _____ _____ my brother is studying now.

시간
❷ I can't remember the year _____ America was discovered.

이유
❸ Sam wanted to know the reason _____ I was so sad.

방법
❹ He will teach us _____ we can swim better.
주의 I don't know the way **how** he made the robot. (○ / ×)

관계부사

복합관계사

1 복합관계대명사

「관계대명사＋-ever」의 형태로, 명사절 또는 양보의 부사절을 이끈다. 복합관계대명사가 이끄는 명사절은 문장에서 주어, 목적어, 보어로 쓰인다.

	명사절	양보의 부사절
whoever	~하는 누구든지 (= anyone who)	누가 ~할지라도 (= No matter who)
whatever	~하는 무엇이든지 (= anything that)	무엇이 ~할지라도 (= No matter what)
whichever	~하는 어느 것이든지 (= anything that)	어느 것이 ~할지라도 (= No matter which)

> 복합관계대명사가 이끄는 명사절이 주어로 쓰인 경우 단수 취급한다.

Whoever made this **is** a great artist. 〈명사절: 주어〉
I believe **whatever** he says. 〈명사절: 목적어〉
You can choose **whichever** you want. 〈명사절: 목적어〉
Whoever comes, don't open the door. 〈양보의 부사절〉
Whatever you do, I'll support you. 〈양보의 부사절〉

2 복합관계부사

「관계부사＋-ever」의 형태로, 장소·시간의 부사절이나 양보의 부사절을 이끈다.

	장소·시간의 부사절	양보의 부사절
wherever	~하는 어디든지, ~하는 곳마다	어디에(서) ~하더라도 (= no matter where)
whenever	~할 때는 언제든지, ~할 때마다	언제 ~하더라도 (= no matter when)
however	—	아무리 ~하더라도 (= no matter how)

Whenever she comes, she brings us presents.
We will find you **wherever** you go.

주의 '아무리 ~하더라도'라는 의미의 양보의 부사절은 「however＋형용사/부사＋주어＋동사」의 어순으로 쓴다.
However hard we try, we won't be able to finish it.

시험 **point**

복합관계부사 however의 어순

양보의 부사절을 이끄는 however 바로 뒤에는 반드시 형용사나 부사가 온다는 사실에 주의한다.

However ⎡ ☐ it is cheap, ⎤ nobody wants it.　　그것이 아무리 싸더라도 아무도 그것을 원하지 않는다.
　　　　　 ⎣ ☑ cheap it is, ⎦

개념 우선 확인 | 밑줄 친 부분의 옳은 해석 고르기

1 <u>Whoever wins</u>, he doesn't care.
- ☐ 누가 이길지라도
- ☐ 이기는 사람은 누구든지

2 Sit <u>wherever you want</u>.
- ☐ 네가 어디를 원하더라도
- ☐ 네가 원하는 곳은 어디든지

3 Buy <u>whatever you need</u>.
- ☐ 네가 필요한 것은 무엇이든지
- ☐ 네가 무엇이 필요할지라도

A 괄호 안에서 알맞은 것을 고르시오.

1 (What / Whatever) he may say, I will not change my mind.

2 In this garden, you will see flowers (where / wherever) you look.

3 (Whoever / Whenever) comes first can choose any seat they want.

4 You must attend the meeting however (you are busy / busy you are).

5 She becomes nervous (whenever / whatever) she has to speak in public.

B 두 문장의 의미가 같도록 빈칸에 알맞은 말을 쓰시오.

1 You can go with anyone who you want.
- → You can go with _____ you want.

2 No matter where you go, you will make new friends.
- → _____ you go, you will make new friends.

3 You can take anything that you want from our refrigerator.
- → You can take _____ you want from our refrigerator.

C 우리말과 일치하도록 괄호 안의 말을 바르게 배열하여 문장을 완성하시오.

1 나는 네가 올 때는 언제든지 환영할 것이다. (come, whenever, you)
- → I will welcome you _____.

2 어제 내가 무슨 말을 하더라도 그는 화를 냈다. (said, whatever, yesterday, I)
- → _____, he got upset.

3 그것이 아무리 비싸더라도 그는 그것을 사고 싶어 했다. (expensive, was, it, however)
- → _____, he wanted to buy it.

30초 완성 map

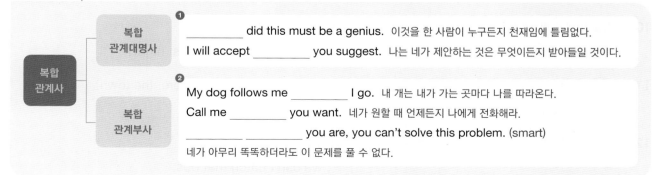

| 복합 관계대명사 | ❶ _____ did this must be a genius. 이것을 한 사람이 누구든지 천재임에 틀림없다.
I will accept _____ you suggest. 나는 네가 제안하는 것은 무엇이든지 받아들일 것이다. |

복합 관계사

| 복합 관계부사 | ❷ My dog follows me _____ I go. 내 개는 내가 가는 곳마다 나를 따라온다.
Call me _____ you want. 네가 원할 때 언제든지 나에게 전화해라.
_____ _____ you are, you can't solve this problem. (smart)
네가 아무리 똑똑하더라도 이 문제를 풀 수 없다. |

서술형 대비 문장 쓰기

Answers p. 18

☐ **빈칸 완성** 괄호 안의 말과 알맞은 관계사를 이용하여 빈칸 완성하기

01 Mike는 그가 공원에서 본 것에 대해 내게 말해 주었다. (see)

→ Mike told me about ＿＿＿＿＿ ＿＿＿＿＿ ＿＿＿＿＿ at the park.

02 그는 모국어가 중국어인 학생들에게 한국어를 가르친다. (native language)

→ He teaches Korean to students ＿＿＿＿＿ ＿＿＿＿＿ ＿＿＿＿＿ is Chinese.

03 우리 부모님은 내가 그분들께 거짓말한 이유를 알고 싶어 하셨다. (the reason)

→ My parents wanted to know ＿＿＿＿＿ ＿＿＿＿＿ ＿＿＿＿＿ I lied to them.

04 내가 그곳에 갈 때마다 비가 많이 온다. (go)

→ ＿＿＿＿＿ ＿＿＿＿＿ ＿＿＿＿＿ there, it rains a lot.

✔ **오류 수정** 어법에 맞게 문장 고쳐 쓰기 (단, 주어진 단어의 순서는 바꾸지 말 것)

05 I love the village where my uncle lives in.

→ I love the village ＿＿＿＿＿＿＿＿＿＿＿＿＿＿＿＿＿＿＿＿ .

06 I don't know the way how they won the match.

→ I don't know ＿＿＿＿＿＿＿＿＿＿＿＿＿＿＿＿＿＿ .

07 Do you have a friend with who you can share everything?

→ Do you have a friend ＿＿＿＿＿＿＿＿＿＿＿＿＿＿＿＿＿＿＿＿ ?

08 He gave me a ticket for the concert, that made me really happy.

→ He gave me a ticket for the concert, ＿＿＿＿＿＿＿＿＿＿＿＿＿＿＿＿＿＿ .

≡ **배열 영작** 괄호 안의 말을 바르게 배열하기

09 이곳이 내가 네게 말했던 그 가게이다. (that, about, I, you, told)

→ This is the store ＿＿＿＿＿＿＿＿＿＿＿＿＿＿＿＿＿＿＿ .

10 이것이 네가 어젯밤에 듣고 있었던 노래니? (to, listening, were, that, you)

→ Is this the song ＿＿＿＿＿＿＿＿＿＿＿＿＿＿＿＿＿＿ last night?

11 지난여름에 나는 나의 아버지가 태어나신 마을에 갔다. (born, my father, was, where, the town)

→ Last summer, I went to ＿＿＿＿＿＿＿＿＿＿＿＿＿＿＿＿＿＿ .

12 우리가 아무리 빨리 뛰더라도 저 버스를 탈 수 없다. (however, run, we, fast)

→ ＿＿＿＿＿＿＿＿＿＿＿＿＿＿＿＿＿＿ , we can't catch that bus.

시험에 꼭 나오는 출제 포인트

Answers p. 19

출제 포인트 ① 관계대명사 what 앞에는 선행사를 쓰지 않는다!

빈칸에 what이 들어갈 수 없는 것은?

① She told me _____ she heard about John.
② I'm thankful for _____ he did for me.
③ Is there anything _____ I can do for you?
④ This is not _____ I expected.
⑤ He didn't understand _____ the teacher said.

출제 포인트 ② 관계대명사를 생략할 수 없는 경우에 주의하자!

밑줄 친 부분 중 생략할 수 없는 것은?

① I know the man who is sitting on the rock.
② She is the woman with whom he is working.
③ The movie which I saw last night was interesting.
④ I lost the umbrella that I bought yesterday.
⑤ These are the photos that were taken in Paris.

출제 포인트 ③ 관계대명사 that은 계속적 용법으로 쓸 수 없다!

어법상 틀린 부분을 찾아 바르게 고쳐 쓰시오.

> I didn't do my homework, that made my
> mom angry.

_____ → _____

> **고득점 POINT** 전치사를 관계대명사 앞에 쓰는 경우에는 관계대명사 that을 쓸 수 없다.
>
> **괄호 안에서 알맞은 것을 고르시오.**
> This is the book for (which / that) you are looking.

출제 포인트 ④ 관계대명사를 쓸지 관계부사를 쓸지 잘 구분하자!

빈칸에 알맞은 말이 순서대로 바르게 짝지어진 것은?

> • This is the house _____ he built 10
>   years ago.
> • April Fools' Day is a day _____
>   everyone can have fun.

> **고득점 POINT** 관계사절에 전치사가 있으면 관계부사를 쓸 수 없다.
>
> **괄호 안에서 알맞은 것을 고르시오.**
> The hotel (which / where) we are staying at is very clean.

① where – when   ② where – which
③ which – when   ④ which – which
⑤ whose – when

실전 Test

[01-03] 다음 빈칸에 들어갈 말로 알맞은 것을 고르시오.
|6점, 각 2점|

01

I like teachers _____ have a sense of humor.

① who   ② whom   ③ which
④ what   ⑤ whose

02

I met a boy _____ name is the same as mine.

① who   ② whom   ③ whose
④ which   ⑤ what

03

She said she was sick yesterday, _____ was not true.

① who   ② what   ③ which
④ when   ⑤ that

04 빈칸에 들어갈 관계대명사가 나머지와 다른 것은? |4점|

① I showed her _____ I had in my hand.
② She got the package _____ I sent her.
③ That's _____ my father needs to buy.
④ She totally forgot _____ I told her.
⑤ _____ is most important is your health.

05 빈칸에 공통으로 들어갈 말로 알맞은 것은? |3점|

• We were having dinner _____ he came back.
• Friday night is the only time _____ I can relax.

① how   ② that   ③ when
④ what   ⑤ where

06 빈칸에 who가 들어갈 수 <u>없는</u> 것은? |3점|

① I saw a man _____ was walking a huge dog.
② Amy, _____ doesn't like sweets, loves ice cream.
③ The boy _____ scored two goals is my brother.
④ She wrote a sweet song, _____ later became a big hit.
⑤ Mr. Lee, _____ is my English teacher, is getting married next week.

최신기출

07 밑줄 친 부분을 생략할 수 있는 문장을 <u>모두</u> 골라 짝지은 것은? |4점|

ⓐ I couldn't believe the story <u>that</u> you told me.
ⓑ The girl <u>who is</u> wearing a red skirt is my little sister.
ⓒ Tell me about the people with <u>whom</u> you work.
ⓓ Look at those puppies <u>that are</u> running in the yard.

① ⓐ, ⓑ   ② ⓑ, ⓓ   ③ ⓐ, ⓑ, ⓓ
④ ⓐ, ⓒ, ⓓ   ⑤ ⓐ, ⓑ, ⓒ, ⓓ

08 밑줄 친 부분과 의미가 같도록 바꿔 쓸 때, 알맞지 <u>않은</u> 것은? |4점|

① Tell me the time <u>when</u> you arrived home.
　　　　　　　　　　　　(→ at which)

② I'm looking for a place <u>where</u> I can stay next week.　　　　(→ for which)

③ He didn't tell me the reason <u>why</u> he loved me.　　　　　　(→ for which)

④ She never forgets the day <u>when</u> her first daughter was born.　　(→ on which)

⑤ Can you remember the garden <u>where</u> we used to play?　　　(→ in which)

09 우리말과 일치하도록 할 때, 빈칸에 들어갈 말로 알맞은 것은? |3점|

그는 내가 먹고 싶은 것을 주문하게 했다.
→ He let me order _____ I wanted to eat.

① it　　　② that　　　③ which
④ what　　⑤ whose

10 어법상 <u>틀린</u> 문장은? |4점|

① This is where the famous singer lives.

② He doesn't know the reason why she left.

③ This is the way how I solved the quiz.

④ The restaurant where we had dinner last night was great.

⑤ Do you know the year when the first Olympics were held?

11 두 문장의 의미가 같도록 할 때, 빈칸에 들어갈 말로 알맞은 것은? |3점|

Anyone who finds the coin first can keep it.
= _____ finds the coin first can keep it.

① Who　　　② What　　　③ Whoever
④ Whatever　⑤ Wherever

12 빈칸에 알맞은 말이 순서대로 바르게 짝지어진 것은? |3점|

• This is the table _____ the movie star had dinner.

• This is the table at _____ the movie star had dinner.

① that – which　　② where – that
③ that – where　　④ which – where
⑤ where – which

고난도
13 빈칸에 들어갈 말로 알맞지 <u>않은</u> 것은? |5점|

The boy _____ is my brother.

① who has blue eyes
② plays soccer
③ dancing on the stage
④ whom Mina likes
⑤ you met yesterday

14 밑줄 친 부분의 쓰임이 <u>어색한</u> 것은? |4점|

① I'll give the prize to <u>whoever</u> arrives first.

② <u>Whatever</u> the decision is, I will follow it.

③ She will like <u>whenever</u> he gives on her birthday.

④ Tom is busy doing something <u>whenever</u> I see him.

⑤ <u>Wherever</u> the singer goes, his fans gather in crowds.

15 밑줄 친 부분의 쓰임이 어법상 옳은 것은? |4점|

① Ms. Choi is one of doctors with who I work.
② He suggested an idea, that was the best one I had heard.
③ Anna, who lives upstairs, brought us a pie.
④ This is that I bought yesterday.
⑤ The problem about that we talked is serious.

16 다음 빈칸 어디에도 들어갈 수 없는 것은? |5점|

ⓐ Italy is the country _____ they want to visit the most.
ⓑ Tell me _____ he left without a word.
ⓒ I will never forget the day _____ I first met him.
ⓓ Can you explain _____ you made the bag?

① where   ② which   ③ why
④ when   ⑤ how

17 우리말과 일치하도록 할 때, 빈칸에 알맞은 말을 모두 고르면? |5점|

네가 아무리 바쁘더라도 끼니를 거르지 마라.
→ _____, don't skip meals.

① How busy you are
② However busy you are
③ However you are busy
④ No matter how you are busy
⑤ No matter how busy you are

18 빈칸에 알맞은 말을 〈보기〉에서 골라 쓰시오. |3점, 각 1점|

| 보기 | which | whose | whom |

(1) Danny has a puppy _____ fur is black.
(2) This is the shop _____ is open 24 hours a day.
(3) Ryan is the man with _____ I play tennis every Saturday.

[19-20] 두 문장을 관계부사를 이용하여 한 문장으로 쓰시오. |4점, 각 2점|

19
• Busan is the city.
• I grew up in the city.

→ Busan is _____
_____ .

20
• I want to know the year.
• You came to Korea in the year.

→ I want to know _____
_____ .

21 대화에서 어법상 틀린 부분을 찾아 바르게 고쳐 쓰시오. (한 단어로 고칠 것) |4점|

A Is this the book you were looking for?
B Yes. It is that I wanted to buy.

_____ → _____

개념 우선 확인 | 옳은 표현 고르기

1 내 가방만큼 큰
- ☐ as big as my bag
- ☐ as bigger as my bag

2 내 신발보다 훨씬 더 큰
- ☐ very bigger than my shoes
- ☐ much bigger than my shoes

3 최고의 가수들 중 한 명
- ☐ one of the best singer
- ☐ one of the best singers

A 괄호 안에서 알맞은 것을 고르시오.

1 Oliver speaks Korean as (well / better) as I do.

2 This sofa is (more comfortable / much comfortable) than that one.

3 This test was (not as / as not) difficult as the last one.

4 This is the (more boring / most boring) movie I have ever seen.

B 밑줄 친 부분을 어법에 맞게 고쳐 쓰시오.

1 Mia is not as <u>older</u> as my sister. Mia is much younger.

2 This smartphone was <u>very</u> more expensive than mine.

3 I think that reading a book is better than <u>watch</u> TV.

4 In Dubai, we visited one of the tallest <u>building</u> in the world.

C 우리말과 일치하도록 괄호 안의 말을 이용하여 문장을 완성하시오.

1 세계에서 가장 큰 대륙은 무엇인가요? (large, continent)

→ What is _____ _____ _____ in the world?

2 그 공연장은 우리 도시에 있는 것보다 훨씬 더 컸다. (far, big)

→ The concert hall was _____ _____ _____ the one in our town.

3 내 남동생의 방은 내 방만큼 깨끗하지 않다. (not, clean)

→ My brother's room is _____ _____ _____ _____ mine.

4 이것은 세계에서 가장 유명한 노래 중 하나이다. (famous, song)

→ This is one of _____ _____ _____ _____ in the world.

30초 완성 map

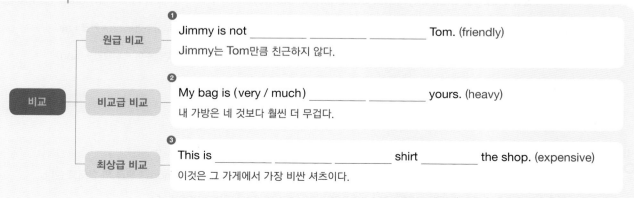

비교

- 원급 비교
  - ❶ Jimmy is not _____ _____ _____ Tom. (friendly)
  Jimmy는 Tom만큼 친근하지 않다.

- 비교급 비교
  - ❷ My bag is (very / much) _____ _____ yours. (heavy)
  내 가방은 네 것보다 훨씬 더 무겁다.

- 최상급 비교
  - ❸ This is _____ _____ _____ shirt _____ the shop. (expensive)
  이것은 그 가게에서 가장 비싼 셔츠이다.

여러 가지 비교 구문

1 배수 비교

몇 배 차이가 나는지를 나타낼 때는 「배수사+as+원급+as」 또는 「배수사+비교급+than」을 쓴다.

New York is	three times	as big as	this city.
		bigger than	

뉴욕은 이 도시의 **세 배만큼 크다**.

뉴욕은 이 도시보다 **세 배 더 크다**.

2 다양한 비교 표현

(1) 비교급+and+비교급: 점점 더 ~한/하게

The tree is growing	**taller and taller**.
Everything will get	**better and better**.

그 나무가 **점점 더 크게** 자라고 있다.

모든 것이 **점점 더 좋아질** 것이다.

(2) the+비교급 ~, the+비교급 ...: 더 ~할수록 더 …하다

	주어+동사		주어+동사
The fresher	the fruit is,	**the better**	it tastes.
The more	you exercise,	**the healthier**	you get.

과일은 **더 신선할수록** 맛이 **더 좋다**.

네가 **더 많이 운동할수록 더 건강해진다**.

(3) as+원급+as possible: 가능한 한 ~한/하게 (= as+원급+as+주어+can)

You should call her	**as soon as possible**.
	as soon as you can.

너는 **가능한 한 빨리** 그녀에게 전화해야 한다.

> 「as+원급+as+주어+can」에서 주어는 주절의 주어를 쓰고, 주절이 과거인 경우에는 could를 쓴다.
> He went to school as early as **he could**.

3 원급과 비교급을 이용한 최상급 표현

Asia is **the largest continent** in the world.	〈the+최상급〉
= Asia is **larger than any other continent** in the world.	〈비교급+than any other+단수명사〉
= **No (other)** continent in the world is **as large as** Asia.	〈부정주어 ~ as+원급+as〉
= **No (other)** continent in the world is **larger than** Asia.	〈부정주어 ~ 비교급+than〉

시험 **point**

「비교급+and+비교급」 구문에서 주의할 점

비교급의 형태가 「more+원급」인 경우, 「비교급+and+비교급」 구문을 「more and more+원급」의 형태로 쓴다.

His song became (more popular and popular / more and more popular).

개념 우선 확인 | 옳은 표현 고르기

1 두 배만큼 무거운
- ☐ two as heavy as
- ☐ twice as heavy as

2 가능한 한 많이
- ☐ as much as possible
- ☐ as possible as much

3 점점 더 큰
- ☐ big and bigger
- ☐ bigger and bigger

A 괄호 안에서 알맞은 것을 고르시오.

1 The hot-air balloon rose (higher or higher / higher and higher).

2 This box is (five times heavier / heavy five times) than that one.

3 We need to finish the work (as quickly as can / as quickly as possible).

4 The more he walked, (the more tired / the most tired) he became.

B 우리말과 일치하도록 괄호 안의 말을 이용하여 문장을 완성하시오.

1 독서를 더 많이 할수록 더 많이 배운다. (much, much)

→ _____ _____ you read, _____ _____ you learn.

2 일자리를 찾는 것이 점점 더 어려워지고 있다. (difficult)

→ It is getting _____ _____ _____ _____ to find a job.

3 이 호텔은 저 호텔보다 세 배만큼 비싸다. (as, expensive)

→ This hotel is _____ _____ _____ _____ _____ that one.

C 〈보기〉의 문장과 의미가 같도록 빈칸에 알맞은 말을 쓰시오.

> 보기　　Seoul is the biggest city in Korea.

1 Seoul is _____ _____ _____ _____ city in Korea.

2 _____ other city in Korea is as _____ as Seoul.

3 _____ other city in Korea is _____ than Seoul.

30초 완성 map

| 배수 비교 | ❶ He is _____ _____ _____ _____ as you. 그는 너의 네 배만큼 나이가 많다. |
| | He is _____ _____ _____ than you. 그는 너보다 나이가 네 배 더 많다. |

| 비교급+and+비교급 | ❷ He ran _____ and _____. (fast) 그는 점점 더 빨리 달렸다. |
| | Surfing is getting _____ and _____ popular. 서핑은 점점 더 인기 있어지고 있다. |

| the+비교급 ~, the+비교급 … | ❸ _____ _____ she grew, _____ _____ she became. (old, wise) 그녀는 더 나이가 들수록 더 현명해졌다. |

| as+원급+as possible | ❹ Come back _____ _____ _____ _____. 가능한 한 빨리 돌아오세요. |

서술형 대비 문장 쓰기

Answers p. 21

빈칸 완성 괄호 안의 말을 이용하여 빈칸 완성하기

01 지구가 점점 더 따뜻해지고 있다. (warm)

→ The earth is getting _____ _____ _____ .

02 그녀는 세계 최고의 축구 선수들 중 한 명이다. (good, soccer player)

→ She is one of _____ _____ _____ _____ in the world.

03 민호는 우리 반에서 다른 어떤 남자아이보다 더 웃기다. (funny, any, boy)

→ Minho is _____ _____ _____ _____ _____ in my class.

04 나는 그들의 노래를 더 많이 들을수록 더 행복해진다. (much, happy)

→ _____ _____ I listen to their songs, _____ _____ I become.

오류 수정 어법에 맞게 문장 고쳐 쓰기

05 Baseball is very more popular than soccer in U.S.

→ Baseball is _____ in U.S.

06 Your hair is nearly three times long than mine.

→ Your hair is nearly _____ mine.

07 His condition became more bad and bad.

→ His condition became _____ .

08 No other island in the world isn't as large as Greenland.

→ No other island in the world _____ .

배열 영작 괄호 안의 말을 바르게 배열하기

09 영화를 보는 것은 게임을 하는 것만큼 재미있지 않다. (playing, as, interesting, not, as)

→ Watching movies is _____ games.

10 수진이는 나보다 훨씬 더 유창하게 영어를 말한다. (do, fluently, much, I, more, than)

→ Sujin speaks English _____ .

11 나는 가능한 한 자주 부모님을 도와드리려고 노력한다. (often, possible, as, as)

→ I try to help my parents _____ .

12 나는 그곳에 더 오래 머무를수록 더 편안하게 느꼈다. (stayed, longer, I, there, the)

→ _____ , the more comfortable I felt.

시험에 꼭 나오는 출제 포인트

Answers p. 21

출제 포인트 **1** 비교급을 강조할 때는 much, even, far, a lot 등을 쓴다!

빈칸에 들어갈 말로 알맞지 않은 것은?

> I can do the work _____ more easily than you can.

① much   ② far   ③ even
④ a lot   ⑤ very

출제 포인트 **2** 비교 표현 다음에 나오는 명사의 수에 주의하자!

밑줄 친 부분이 어법상 틀린 것은?

① Minho is the oldest of our club's members.
② This is one of the longest river in the world.
③ Michael swims the fastest of the three.
④ No fantasy novel is more interesting than this one.
⑤ August is hotter than any other month of the year.

출제 포인트 **3** 「the + 비교급 + 주어 + 동사, the + 비교급 + 주어 + 동사」의 어순에 주의하자!

우리말과 일치하도록 괄호 안의 말을 배열하여 문장을 완성하시오.

> 네가 더 빨리 걸을수록 더 일찍 도착할 것이다.
> (sooner, you, the, arrive, will)

→ The faster you walk, _____

_____ .

> **고득점 POINT** 「more + 형용사/부사」 형태의 비교급인 경우, more와 형용사를 분리해서 쓰지 않도록 주의한다.
>
> **어법상 틀린 부분을 찾아 바르게 고쳐 쓰시오.**
>
> The bigger a house is, the more it is expensive.
> → The bigger a house is, _____ .

출제 포인트 **4** 최상급의 의미를 나타내는 다양한 표현을 익혀 두자!

문장의 의미가 나머지와 다른 것은?

① Jim is the tallest boy in the class.
② No boy in the class is as tall as Jim.
③ No boy in the class is taller than Jim.
④ Jim is as tall as all the other boys in the class.
⑤ Jim is taller than any other boy in the class.

> **고득점 POINT** 부정주어를 사용하여 최상급을 표현할 때 동사에 not을 쓰지 않도록 주의한다.
>
> **다음 중 어법상 틀린 것을 찾아 기호를 쓰고, 바르게 고쳐 쓰시오.**
>
> No one in the world ⓐdoesn't play the violin as ⓑwell ⓒas Ms. Park.
> (_____) → _____

[01-03] 다음 빈칸에 들어갈 말로 알맞은 것을 고르시오.

|6점, 각 2점|

01

He speaks English _____ than his parents do.

① good   ② well   ③ better
④ best   ⑤ the most

02

Your bag is _____ as heavy as mine.

① two   ② second   ③ the second
④ twice   ⑤ two time

03

This game is _____ game that I have ever played.

① exciting   ② more exciting
③ most exciting   ④ the more exciting
⑤ the most exciting

04 빈칸에 들어갈 말이 나머지와 다른 것은? |3점|

① Mr. Lee is the richest person _____ Korea.
② David is the youngest _____ the three children.
③ This house is the cheapest _____ the town.
④ This is the most comfortable chair _____ the room.
⑤ They sell the most delicious muffins _____ the village.

05 밑줄 친 부분과 바꿔 쓸 수 있는 것은? |3점|

This watch is four times as expensive as that one.

① as four times as expensive than
② four more expensive than
③ four more times expensive than
④ more expensive than four times
⑤ four times more expensive than

06 다음 중 의미가 나머지와 다른 것은? |4점|

① The blue whale is the largest animal in the world.
② The blue whale is larger than any other animal in the world.
③ The blue whale is as large as all the other animals in the world.
④ No animal in the world is as large as the blue whale.
⑤ No animal in the world is larger than the blue whale.

07 빈칸에 알맞은 말이 순서대로 바르게 짝지어진 것은? |4점|

_____ the fruit is, _____ it is.

① Fresh – tasty
② The fresh – the tasty
③ The fresher – the tastier
④ The more fresh – the more tasty
⑤ The most fresh – the most tasty

08 다음 중 어법상 <u>틀린</u> 문장은? |4점|

① My cat is much faster than my dog.
② This picture is not as unique as yours.
③ Einstein was one of the greatest scientists in history.
④ Playing soccer is more exciting than watching it on TV.
⑤ This is the more difficult project that I have ever done.

09 (A)~(C)에 들어갈 말이 바르게 짝지어진 것은? |4점|

• My car is not as large as (A) you / yours .
• Mt. Halla is higher than any other
  (B) mountain / mountains in South Korea.
• Mr. Cho is one of the most famous
  (C) pianist / pianists in the world.

	(A)	(B)	(C)
①	you	mountain	pianists
②	you	mountains	pianist
③	yours	mountain	pianist
④	yours	mountain	pianists
⑤	yours	mountains	pianists

10 우리말을 영어로 옮길 때, 알맞지 <u>않은</u> 것은? |5점|

① 그것은 가장 쉬운 방법 중 하나이다.
→ It is one of the easiest ways.
② 토끼는 거북보다 훨씬 더 빠르다.
→ The rabbit is far faster than the turtle.
③ 이 규칙은 다른 어떤 규칙보다 더 중요하다.
→ This rule is more important than any other rule.
④ 그녀는 가능한 한 조심스럽게 운전했다.
→ She drove more carefully as she could.
⑤ 그 소고기는 내가 지금껏 먹어 본 중 최고의 고기였다.
→ The beef was the best meat I have ever eaten.

11 우리말과 일치하도록 괄호 안의 말을 배열할 때, 여섯 번째로 오는 단어는? |4점|

나는 더 열심히 연습할수록 더 잘 노래했다.
(practiced, harder, I, the, better, I, sang, the)

① harder ② sang ③ I
④ better ⑤ practiced

12 우리말과 일치하도록 할 때, 빈칸에 알맞은 것은? |3점|

이 수학 수업은 점점 더 어려워지고 있다.
→ This math class is getting _____ difficult.

① much ② more
③ difficult and ④ more and more
⑤ much and much

13 다음 빈칸에 들어갈 수 <u>없는</u> 것은? |3점|

Today is _____ colder than yesterday.

① very ② far ③ much
④ even ⑤ a lot

14 짝지어진 두 문장의 의미가 서로 <u>다른</u> 것은? |4점|

① Walk as fast as you can.
= Walk as fast as possible.
② Hobin is taller than Yumi.
= Yumi is not as tall as Hobin.
③ This book is much thicker than that one.
= This book is far thicker than that one.
④ She is the fastest skater in the world.
= She is faster than any other skater in the world.
⑤ No other student in my school is as polite as Minho.
= Minho isn't as polite as other students in my school.

15 빈칸에 more를 쓸 수 <u>없는</u> 것은? |3점|

① I read _____ than he does.

② My brother eats almost three times _____ than me.

③ These pants are _____ comfortable than mine.

④ The more he talked, the _____ bored I became.

⑤ Try to laugh as _____ as possible.

고난도

16 어법상 옳은 문장의 개수는? |5점|

ⓐ This tree is twice as taller as the house.

ⓑ Please let me know the results as soon as possible.

ⓒ His headache is getting more serious and serious.

ⓓ Nothing isn't as important as my friends to me.

① 없음 　　② 1개 　　③ 2개
④ 3개 　　⑤ 4개

최신기출 고난도

17 각 빈칸에 들어갈 말로 알맞지 <u>않은</u> 것은? |5점|

• Jiwoo is smarter _____ ⓐ _____ .

• The more you study, _____ ⓑ _____ .

• Please send me an email _____ ⓒ _____ .

• The little boy is becoming _____ ⓓ _____ .

• My father works for one of _____ ⓔ _____ .

① ⓐ – than any other girl in my class

② ⓑ – your grades will be the better

③ ⓒ – as soon as you can

④ ⓓ – healtheir and healthier

⑤ ⓔ – the biggest companies in Korea

18 빈칸에 들어갈 말을 〈보기〉에서 골라 알맞은 형태로 쓰시오. |3점, 각 1점|

| 보기 | bad | intelligent | high |

(1) My score is much _____ than yours.

(2) This is the _____ movie that I have ever seen.

(3) Mike is not as _____ as his brother.

[19-20] 다음 정보를 보고, 괄호 안의 말을 이용하여 문장을 완성하시오. (필요하면 형태를 바꿀 것) |8점, 각 4점|

19

Sarah spent $100 last month.

Julie spent $300 last month.

→ Julie spent _____ Sarah did last month. (three, much, than)

20

The weight of the red bike is 12 kg.

The weight of the blue bike is 14 kg.

→ The red bike is _____ the blue one. (heavy, as)

21 어법상 <u>틀린</u> 부분을 찾아 바르게 고쳐 쓰시오. |4점|

Today is one of the coldest day of the year.
(오늘은 올해 가장 추운 날들 중 하나이다.)

_____ → _____

1 If I had more time, I could do better.
- ☐ 시간이 없어서 더 잘할 수 없다
- ☐ 시간이 있어서 더 잘할 수 있다

2 If she had tried harder, she could have won.
- ☐ 더 열심히 노력하여 이길 수 있었다
- ☐ 더 열심히 노력하지 않아서 이길 수 없었다

A 괄호 안에서 알맞은 것을 고르시오.

1 If I felt better, I (will go / would go) hiking with you.

2 If I (am / were) you, I would never do that.

3 If we (had / had had) enough time, we could have visited the museum.

4 If you had studied harder, you (could pass / could have passed) the exam.

B 밑줄 친 부분을 어법에 맞게 고쳐 쓰시오.

1 If I knew her email address, I will send her the pictures.

2 If my grandfather is still alive, he would be 99 this year.

3 If he had driven more carefully, he wouldn't have a car accident.

4 If you don't lie to her, she wouldn't have been angry with you.

C 주어진 문장을 가정법으로 바꿔 쓸 때, 빈칸에 알맞은 말을 쓰시오.

1 As I don't have enough money, I can't buy this bike.
→ If I _____ enough money, I _____ _____ this bike.

2 As Suji is not here, we aren't having fun.
→ If Suji _____ here, we _____ _____ having fun.

3 Because we did not leave earlier, we missed the train.
→ If we _____ _____ earlier, we wouldn't _____ _____ the train.

4 As they didn't ask for help, I didn't help them.
→ If they _____ _____ for help, I _____ _____ _____ them.

30초 완성 map

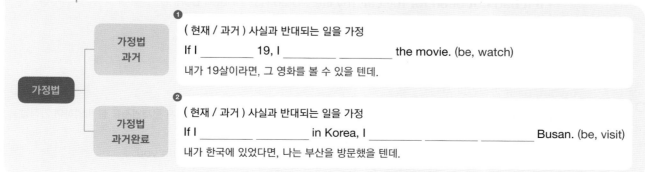

❶ (현재 / 과거) 사실과 반대되는 일을 가정
If I _____ 19, I _____ _____ the movie. (be, watch)
내가 19살이라면, 그 영화를 볼 수 있을 텐데.

❷ (현재 / 과거) 사실과 반대되는 일을 가정
If I _____ _____ in Korea, I _____ _____ Busan. (be, visit)
내가 한국에 있었다면, 나는 부산을 방문했을 텐데.

가정법 — 가정법 과거 / 가정법 과거완료

I wish, as if, without(but for)

1 I wish 가정법

이루기 힘든 현재의 소망이나 과거에 이루지 못한 일에 대한 아쉬움을 나타낼 때 쓴다.

I wish	가정법 과거 (주어+동사의 과거형) (현재) ~한다면 좋을 텐데	I wish you **were** here. (→ I'm sorry that you **are not** here.)
	가정법 과거완료 (주어+had+p.p.) (과거에) ~했다면 좋을 텐데	I wish you **had been** there. (→ I'm sorry that you **were not** there.)

2 as if 가정법

현재나 과거 사실과 반대되는 내용을 가정하며 '실제로 그렇지 않지만 그런 척한다'라는 의미를 나타낼 때 쓴다.

as if	가정법 과거 (주어+동사의 과거형) 마치 ~한 것처럼	He talks **as if** he **knew** everything. (→ In fact, he **doesn't know** everything.)
	가정법 과거완료 (주어+had+p.p.) 마치 ~했던 것처럼	He talks **as if** he **had known** everything. (→ In fact, he **didn't know** everything.)

3 without(but for)+명사(구): ~이 없(었)다면

가정법의 if절을 대신하는 구문으로 뒤에 가정법 과거와 가정법 과거완료를 쓸 수 있다.

Without your help, = **But for** your help,	I **would fail**.	〈가정법 과거〉 네 도움이 **없다면**, 나는 실패할 텐데.
	I **would have failed**.	〈가정법 과거완료〉 네 도움이 **없었다면**, 나는 실패했을 텐데.

> without(but for) 구문은 if절로 바꿔 쓸 수 있는데, 주절이 가정법 과거이면 If it were not for ~로, 가정법 과거완료이면 If it had not been for ~로 바꿔 쓸 수 있다.

Without my cat, my life would be boring.
→ **If it were not for** my cat, my life would be boring.

Without my cat, my life would have been boring.
→ **If it had not been for** my cat, my life would have been boring.

시험
point

I wish, as if 가정법의 시제

I wish와 as if 다음에는 가정법 과거와 가정법 과거완료가 모두 올 수 있으므로, 과거인지 현재인지를 잘 파악하여 가정법 과거를 쓸지 가정법 과거완료를 쓸지 판단한다.

1 그곳에 너와 같이 갔다면 좋을 텐데. → I wish I (went / had gone) there with you.

2 그는 마치 자신이 부자인 것처럼 말한다. → He talks as if he (were / had been) rich.

1 I wish I lived in Paris.
- ☐ 현재 파리에 산다
- ☐ 현재 파리에 살지 않는다

2 He talks as if he were a doctor.
- ☐ 그는 의사이다
- ☐ 그는 의사가 아니다

3 Without you, I would be lonely.
- ☐ 네가 있어서 나는 외롭지 않다
- ☐ 네가 없어서 나는 외롭다

A 괄호 안에서 알맞은 것을 고르시오.

1 I don't have a pet. I wish I (have / had) a dog.

2 He acts as if he (were / had been) my boyfriend. But he wasn't.

3 Without electricity, our lives (would be / would have been) very different now.

B 우리말과 일치하도록 괄호 안의 말을 알맞은 형태로 바꿔 쓰시오.

1 내가 작년에 돈을 더 모았다면 좋을 텐데. (save)

→ I wish I _____ more money last year.

2 그의 조언이 없었다면, 나는 곤경에 처했었을 텐데. (be)

→ Without his advice, I _____ in trouble.

3 그녀는 마치 자신이 나의 엄마인 것처럼 말한다. (be)

→ She talks as if she _____ my mom.

C 주어진 문장과 의미가 같도록 가정법 문장을 완성하시오.

1 In fact, he is surprised at the news.

→ He acts _____ at the news.

2 I'm sorry that I was not a famous musician.

→ _____ a famous musician.

3 If it had not been for your present, Sue would have been disappointed.

→ _____, Sue would have been disappointed.

30초 완성 map

I wish 가정법

I wish he _____ here with us. (be)　　　　그가 이곳에 우리와 같이 있다면 좋을 텐데.

I wish he _____ _____ here with us.　　그가 이곳에 우리와 같이 있었다면 좋을 텐데.

as if 가정법

He talks **as if** he _____ the answer. (know)　　그는 마치 답을 아는 것처럼 말한다.

He talks **as if** he _____ _____ the answer.　그는 마치 답을 알았던 것처럼 말한다.

without (but for) + 명사(구)

Without your help, we _____ _____ problems. (have)

네 도움이 없다면, 우리는 문제가 생길 텐데.

Without your help, we _____ _____ _____ problems.

네 도움이 없었다면, 우리는 문제가 생겼을 텐데.

↻ 문장 전환 의미가 같도록 가정법 문장으로 바꿔 쓰기

01 As I don't have the key, I can't open the door.

→ If I _____ the key, I _____ the door.

02 I am sorry you didn't eat breakfast this morning.

→ I wish you _____ breakfast this morning.

03 As he forgot her birthday, she was angry.

→ If he _____ her birthday, she _____ angry.

04 As the weather was not good yesterday, we couldn't go to the beach.

→ If the weather _____ good yesterday, we _____ to the beach.

✓ 오류 수정 어법에 맞게 밑줄 친 부분 고쳐 쓰기

05 If he doesn't have homework, he could go with us.

→ _____, he could go with us.

06 If I have more time, I could have done better.

→ _____, I could have done better.

07 Tom acts as if he had been the leader of our team. But he isn't.

→ Tom acts as if _____. But he isn't.

08 I wish I buy the sneakers yesterday. They were on sale.

→ I wish _____ yesterday. They were on sale.

☐ 빈칸 완성 괄호 안의 말을 이용하여 빈칸 완성하기

09 내가 너라면, 그녀와 함께 영화를 보러 갈 텐데. (be, go)

→ If I _____ you, I _____ to the movies with her.

10 그는 마치 그가 사고를 봤던 것처럼 말한다. (see)

→ He talks as if he _____ the accident.

11 네가 주의했었다면, 그런 실수를 하지 않았을 텐데. (be, make)

→ If you _____ careful, you _____ such a mistake.

12 이 만화책들이 없었다면, 나는 매우 따분했을 텐데. (be)

→ Without these comic books, I _____ very bored.

시험에 꼭 나오는 출제 포인트

Answers p. 23

출제 포인트 ① 가정법 과거와 가정법 과거완료의 형태를 잘 기억하자!

빈칸에 들어갈 말로 알맞은 것은?

> If I were not busy, I _____ the club.

① join　　　　　② joined
③ will join　　　④ would join
⑤ would have joined

고득점 POINT 가정법 과거완료의 형태

우리말과 일치하도록 괄호 안의 말을 알맞은 형태로 바꿔 쓰시오.

내게 충분한 돈이 있었다면, 나는 그 청바지를 샀을 텐데.
(have, will, buy)

→ If I _____ enough money, I _____
_____ the jeans.

출제 포인트 ② 가정법 과거는 현재 사실의 반대, 가정법 과거완료는 과거 사실의 반대를 가정한다!

두 문장의 의미가 같도록 문장을 완성하시오.

(1) As you don't have the car key, you can't get in the car.

→ If you _____ the car key, you _____ in the car.

(2) As she didn't call me, I got worried.

→ If she _____ me, I _____ worried.

출제 포인트 ③ I wish 가정법과 as if 가정법의 형태에 주의하자!

빈칸에 들어갈 말로 알맞은 것은?

> I wish we _____ to the concert last night.

① go　　　　　② went
③ had gone　　④ will go
⑤ would go

고득점 POINT as if + 가정법 과거완료

우리말과 일치하도록 주어진 말을 알맞은 형태로 쓰시오.

그는 마치 자신이 유명했던 것처럼 말한다.
→ He talks as if he _____ famous. (be)

출제 포인트 ④ without 구문은 주절의 시제에 따라 가정법의 시제가 결정된다는 점에 주의하자!

두 문장의 의미가 같도록 할 때, 빈칸에 알맞은 말을 쓰시오.

> Without you, I would have given up my dream.

→ If it _____ _____ _____ _____ you, I would have given up my dream.

유형	문항수	배점	점수
객관식	17	55	
서술형	10	45	

[01-03] 다음 빈칸에 들어갈 말로 알맞은 것을 고르시오.
|6점, 각 2점|

01
If I won the lottery, I _____ a nice car.

① buy ② bought
③ will buy ④ would buy
⑤ would have bought

02
If I _____ a cat, I would have named it Kitty.

① had ② have
③ have had ④ had had
⑤ will have

03
I wish I _____ good at swimming.

① am ② were
③ has been ④ will be
⑤ would be

04 빈칸에 알맞은 be동사의 형태가 나머지와 다른 것은?
|4점|

① If he _____ in Seoul, he could come to my graduation.
② If I _____ there yesterday, I could have seen him.
③ You have a test tomorrow. If I _____ you, I would study hard.
④ If I _____ over 18 years old, I could watch the movie.
⑤ I wish Tom and I _____ in the same class. But we are in different classes.

05 빈칸에 공통으로 들어갈 말로 알맞은 것은?
|3점|

• If you _____ a billion dollars, what would you do with it?
• I'm an only child. I wish I _____ a brother.

① have ② had ③ had had
④ will have ⑤ would have

[06-07] 우리말과 일치하도록 할 때, 빈칸에 들어갈 말로 알맞은 것을 고르시오.
|4점, 각 2점|

06
그는 마치 프랑스에서 살았던 것처럼 말한다.
→ He talks as if he _____ in France.

① live ② lived
③ lives ④ has lived
⑤ had lived

07
그녀가 그렇게 많은 돈을 쓰지 않았다면 좋을 텐데.
→ I wish she _____ so much money.

① spent ② doesn't spend
③ didn't spend ④ had spent
⑤ had not spent

[08-09] 다음 중 밑줄 친 부분이 어법상 틀린 것을 고르시오.

|8점, 각 4점|

08 ① I wish I <u>have</u> big eyes.

② I wish today <u>were</u> Friday.

③ My aunt treats me as if I <u>were</u> her own child.

④ Jane always talks as if she <u>knew</u> everything.

⑤ Where would you go if you <u>had</u> some time?

09 ① If I <u>had not missed</u> the train, I would have met her.

② If you <u>don't invite</u> him, he would have been disappointed.

③ Without coffee, I <u>couldn't have stayed</u> up late last night.

④ If I had watered the flowers, they <u>would not have died</u>.

⑤ If you <u>had not moved</u> to this city, I couldn't have met you.

10 주어진 문장을 가정법 문장으로 바꿀 때, 빈칸에 알맞은 말이 순서대로 바르게 짝지어진 것은? |4점|

As it is cold today, we can't play outside.

→ If it _____ cold today, we _____ ouside.

① was – could play

② were – could play

③ were – couldn't play

④ weren't – could play

⑤ weren't – couldn't play

11 다음 우리말을 영작할 때, 필요하지 <u>않은</u> 단어는? |4점|

내가 너였다면, 그것을 사지 않았을 텐데.

① had   ② buy   ③ have

④ been   ⑤ wouldn't

12 주어진 문장에서 알 수 있는 사실로 알맞은 것은? |3점|

He speaks as if he were an American.

① He is an American.

② He is not an American.

③ He was an American.

④ He was not an American.

⑤ He must be an American.

13 두 문장의 의미가 같도록 할 때, 빈칸에 들어갈 말로 알맞은 것은? |3점|

I'm sorry that I didn't listen to my parents when I was young.

→ I wish I _____ to my parents when I was young.

① listen   ② listened

③ didn't listen   ④ had listened

⑤ had not listened

14 밑줄 친 부분과 바꿔 쓸 수 있는 것은? |3점|

If it <u>had not been for</u> your advice, we might have lost the game.

① But   ② I wish

③ With   ④ Without

⑤ Although

15 밑줄 친 문장에서 어법상 틀린 부분을 찾아 바르게 고친 것은? |5점|

> People said that last night's party was amazing. <u>I wish I went to it.</u>

① wish → wished
② wish → had wished
③ went → go
④ went → had gone
⑤ went → have been

16 (A)~(C)에 들어갈 말이 바르게 짝지어진 것은? |4점|

> • What (A) [did / would] happen if I pressed the red button?
> • If I hadn't lost my phone, I could (B) [call / have called] you earlier.
> • If the road (C) [weren't / hadn't been] wet, he wouldn't have crashed his car.

	(A)	(B)	(C)
①	did	call	weren't
②	did	have called	weren't
③	would	call	hadn't been
④	would	have called	hadn't been
⑤	would	have called	weren't

17 밑줄 친 부분이 어법상 옳은 것을 모두 골라 짝지은 것은? |4점|

> ⓐ He acts as if he <u>were</u> a doctor.
> ⓑ If I had been home, I <u>wouldn't have been</u> so cold.
> ⓒ If I <u>have driven</u> my car, I could have arrived earlier.
> ⓓ If I knew her, I <u>can introduce</u> her to you.

① ⓐ, ⓑ
② ⓑ, ⓒ
③ ⓒ, ⓓ
④ ⓐ, ⓑ, ⓒ
⑤ ⓐ, ⓑ, ⓒ, ⓓ

서술형

[18-19] 다음 문장을 가정법으로 바꿀 때, 빈칸에 알맞은 말을 쓰시오. |6점, 각 3점|

18

> As I didn't do my homework, Mom was angry at me.

→ If I _____ _____ my homework, Mom _____ not _____ _____ angry at me.

19

> I'm sorry that your bike is broken.

→ I wish your bike _____ _____ _____ .

20 그림을 보고, 여자가 할 말을 괄호 안의 말을 이용하여 가정법 문장으로 쓰시오. |3점|

→ If I _____ a dog, I _____ very happy now. (have, be, will)

개념 우선 확인 | **옳은 문장 고르기**

1 내가 그를 본 곳은 바로 이곳이었다.
- ☐ I saw him here.
- ☐ It was here that I saw him.

2 나는 그것을 정말로 끝냈다.
- ☐ I do finish it.
- ☐ I did finish it.

3 여기 기차가 온다.
- ☐ Here comes the train.
- ☐ Here the train comes.

A 괄호 안에서 알맞은 것을 고르시오.

1 I did (give / gave) you the key, right?

2 (There / It) was on the subway that I lost my wallet.

3 On the wall (was / were) some pictures that he had painted.

4 Kate doesn't enjoy going shopping. (So / Neither) does Mia.

B 밑줄 친 부분을 어법에 맞게 고쳐 쓰시오. (단, 단어를 없애지 말 것)

1 There <u>your sister goes</u>.

2 Next to their house <u>was</u> some big trees.

3 I <u>did turned off</u> the computer last night after using it.

4 I really like watching horror movies. <u>So does Ben and Joe</u>.

C 밑줄 친 부분을 강조하는 문장으로 바꿔 쓰시오.

1 <u>My brother</u> ate the whole cake.
→ It _____ ate the whole cake.

2 He <u>remembered</u> the place where he took these photos.
→ _____ where he took these photos.

3 Andy bought her <u>a ring</u> for her birthday.
→ It _____ Andy bought her for her birthday.

30초 완성 map

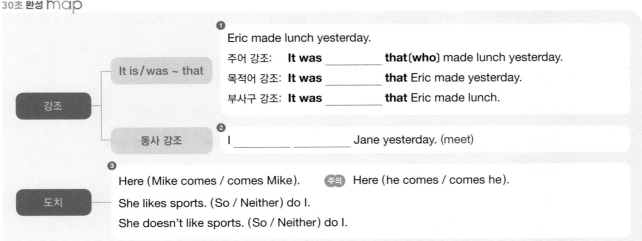

❶ Eric made lunch yesterday.

It is/was ~ that

주어 강조: **It was** _____ **that(who)** made lunch yesterday.
목적어 강조: **It was** _____ **that** Eric made yesterday.
부사구 강조: **It was** _____ **that** Eric made lunch.

동사 강조

❷ I _____ _____ Jane yesterday. (meet)

❸ 도치

Here (Mike comes / comes Mike).   주의 Here (he comes / comes he).

She likes sports. (So / Neither) do I.

She doesn't like sports. (So / Neither) do I.

화법

직접화법은 다른 사람이 한 말을 큰따옴표로 묶어서 그대로 전달하는 것이고, 간접화법은 큰따옴표를 쓰지 않고 전달자의 입장에 맞게 바꿔서 전달하는 것이다.

1 평서문의 화법 전환

직접화법	She	said to	me,		"You	look	great	today."
간접화법	She	**told**	me	**that**	**I**	**looked**	great	**that day**.
		①		②	③	④		⑤

① 전달동사를 바꾼다. (say → say, say to → tell)
② 콤마(,)와 큰따옴표를 없애고 접속사 that을 쓴다. (that은 생략 가능)
③ that절의 인칭대명사를 전달자에 맞춰 바꾼다.
④ that절의 동사는 주절의 시제에 일치시킨다.
⑤ 지시어나 부사(구)를 상황에 맞게 바꾼다.

> 간접화법으로 전환 시 바뀌는 부사(구)
> this → that   these → those
> now → then   ago → before
> today → that day
> yesterday → the day before
> tomorrow → the next day

▶ 주절의 시제가 과거일 때 큰따옴표 안이 과거이면 간접화법에서 과거완료로 바꾼다.

She **said** to me, "I **saw** you at the park."
→ She told me that she **had seen** me at the park.

2 의문문의 화법 전환

(1) 의문사가 있는 의문문: 의문문을 「의문사＋주어＋동사」의 어순으로 바꾼다.

직접화법	Mom asked me,	"Where	are	you?"
간접화법	Mom asked me	where	**I**	**was**.

▶ 의문사가 주어인 경우에는 「의문사＋동사」의 어순을 그대로 쓴다.
Kevin asked me **who made** the cake.

(2) 의문사가 없는 의문문: 의문문을 「if〔whether〕＋주어＋동사」의 어순으로 바꾼다.

직접화법	He asked me,	"Do	you	need	more time?"
간접화법	He asked me	**if〔whether〕**	**I**	**needed**	more time.

3 명령문의 화법 전환

전달동사를 tell, order, advise, ask, warn 등으로 바꾸고, 명령문을 to부정사로 바꾼다.

직접화법	The doctor said to him,	"Exercise	regularly."
간접화법	The doctor **advised** him	**to exercise**	regularly.

▶ 부정 명령문인 경우에는 to 앞에 not을 붙인다.
She said to me, "Don't sit on the chair."
→ She **warned** me **not to sit** on the chair.

개념 우선 확인 | 옳은 문장 고르기

1 그는 매우 피곤하다고 말했다.
- ☐ He said I was very tired.
- ☐ He said he was very tired.

2 그는 나에게 어디에 있는지 물었다.
- ☐ He asked me where was I.
- ☐ He asked me where I was.

3 그는 우리에게 오라고 말했다.
- ☐ He told us to come.
- ☐ He said that we come.

A 직접화법을 간접화법으로 바꿀 때, 괄호 안에서 알맞은 것을 고르시오.

1 She said to me, "I want to come with you."
→ She told me that (I / she) wanted to come with (you / me).

2 John asked me, "Are you busy?"
→ John asked me (that / if) I was busy.

3 I asked him, "Where do you live?"
→ I asked him where (did he live / he lived).

B 밑줄 친 부분을 어법에 맞게 고쳐 쓰시오.

1 He said me that he had bought a new watch.

2 She asked me what was my name.

3 He ordered us don't enter the room.

C 직접화법을 간접화법으로 바꾼 문장을 완성하시오.

1 I asked him, "When were you born?"
→ I asked him _____.

2 Sujin asked me, "Do you want to join us?"
→ Sujin asked me _____.

3 Mr. Brown said to the students, "Don't make any noise."
→ Mr. Brown told _____.

30초 완성 map

화법 전환

평서문
❶ He said to me, "I have a test today."
→ He _____ me that _____ _____ a test that day.

의문문
❷ He asked me, "Where are you?"
→ He asked me _____ _____ _____.
He asked me, "Do you want a drink?"
→ He asked me _____ _____ _____ a drink.

명령문
❸ He said to me, "Come to the party."
→ He told me _____ _____ to the party.

서술형 대비 문장 쓰기

≡ 배열 영작 괄호 안의 말을 바르게 배열하기

01 그가 중학교를 졸업한 것은 바로 작년이었다. (was, last, that, year, graduated, he, it)

→ _____ from middle school.

02 그 경찰관은 나에게 어디에서 그 이상한 남자를 봤는지 물었다. (the, had, where, strange, I, man, seen)

→ The police officer asked me _____.

03 선생님께서는 우리에게 수업 중에 전화기를 사용하지 말라고 말씀하셨다. (to, told, use, us, not, our phones)

→ Our teacher _____ during class.

04 나는 어제 네 책을 네 책상 위에 정말 두었다. (put, your, did, book)

→ I _____ on your desk yesterday.

↻ 문장 전환 지시에 맞게 문장 바꿔 쓰기

05 She said to me, "I met Mike yesterday." (간접화법으로)

→ She _____.

06 Sam asked me, "Why are you late for school?" (간접화법으로)

→ Sam asked me _____.

07 The concert took place in Seoul. (in Seoul을 강조하여)

→ It _____.

08 A man stood in front of the door. (in front of the door로 시작하는 문장으로)

→ _____

✓ 오류 수정 어법에 맞게 문장 고쳐 쓰기

09 Here the novels that you wanted are.

→ Here _____.

10 He asked me what time was it.

→ He asked me _____.

11 It was my umbrella that I lost it on the bus.

→ It was my umbrella that _____.

12 John didn't enjoy the game. So did I. It was boring.

→ John didn't enjoy the game. _____ It was boring.

시험에 나오는 출제 포인트

출제 포인트 ① It is / was ~ that 강조 구문의 쓰임에 주의하자!

밑줄 친 부분의 쓰임이 나머지와 다른 것은?

① It is Mina that he likes.
② It is this bag that I want to buy.
③ It was yesterday that she met him.
④ It is certain that he will pass the exam.
⑤ It was in the park that I lost my wallet.

> **고특점 POINT** 동사를 강조하는 do동사
>
> **밑줄 친 부분을 강조하여 문장을 다시 쓰시오.**
>
> I sent you an email last week.
>
> → I _____ you an email last week.

출제 포인트 ② 도치 구문에서 동사는 뒤에 나오는 주어에 일치시켜야 한다!

어법상 틀린 부분을 찾아 바르게 고쳐 쓰시오.

> Under the tree was some comfortable chairs.

_____ → _____

출제 포인트 ③ 「So/Neither + 동사 + 주어」의 어순에 주의하자!

괄호 안의 말을 바르게 배열하여 대화를 완성하시오.

(1) **A** Ann is 15 years old.

   B _____ (I, am, so)

(2) **A** I don't like horror movies.

   B _____

   (my brother, neither, does)

> **고특점 POINT** 「So/Neither + 동사 + 주어」에서 동사의 형태는 앞 문장의 동사에 의해 결정된다.
>
> **괄호 안에서 알맞은 것을 고르시오.**
>
> (1) **A** I went shopping yesterday.
>   **B** So (do / did) I.
>
> (2) **A** She can't speak English fluently.
>   **B** Neither (do / can) I.

출제 포인트 ④ 직접화법을 간접화법으로 바꿀 때는 전달동사, 대명사, 시제에 주의한다!

직접화법을 간접화법으로 바꾼 문장에서 어법상 틀린 부분을 찾아 기호를 쓰고 바르게 고쳐 쓰시오.

> Tom said to me, "I like your gift."
> → Tom ⓐ told me ⓑ that ⓒ I ⓓ liked ⓔ my gift.

( ) → _____

[01-02] 다음 빈칸에 들어갈 말로 알맞은 것을 고르시오.

|4점, 각 2점|

01

It was Peter _____ gave me this cap on my birthday.

① do　　　② if　　　③ which
④ that　　　⑤ what

02

In front of the station _____ many stores.

① is　　　② are　　　③ be
④ do　　　⑤ does

[03-05] 다음 문장을 간접화법으로 바꿀 때, 빈칸에 알맞은 말을 고르시오.

|9점, 각 3점|

03

Junho said to me, "I will visit you tomorrow."
→ Junho told me that _____
　　the next day.

① I will visit him
② I would visit you
③ I would visit him
④ he would visit me
⑤ he would visit you

04

He said to me, "What is your dream?"
→ He asked me _____ .

① what is my dream
② what my dream was
③ what was my dream
④ what your dream is
⑤ what your dream was

05

She said to us, "Be quiet here."
→ She asked us _____ there.

① quiet　　　② be quiet
③ to quiet　　　④ to be quiet
⑤ to do quiet

06 다음 문장의 일부를 강조한 문장으로 알맞지 <u>않은</u> 것은?

|4점|

Ted met Sally in the library last week.

① It was Ted that met Sally in the library last week.
② It was the library that Ted met Sally last week.
③ It was last week that Ted met Sally in the library.
④ It was in the library that Ted met Sally last week.
⑤ It was Sally that Ted met in the library last week.

07 밑줄 친 부분을 강조하는 문장으로 바꿔 쓸 때, 빈칸에 들어갈 말로 알맞은 것은?

|3점|

I <u>told</u> you about it yesterday.
→ I _____ you about it yesterday.

① told do　　　② tell did　　　③ did tell
④ did told　　　⑤ do told

08 빈칸에 are를 쓸 수 <u>없는</u> 것은? |4점|

① Here _____ the books you asked for.
② Beyond the woods _____ their house.
③ On the table _____ the old magazines.
④ Around the corner _____ some popular restaurants.
⑤ In the classroom _____ ten students waiting for the teacher.

09 다음 문장을 간접화법으로 바르게 바꾼 것은? |4점|

The captain said to us, "Don't step back."

① The captain warned us not step back.
② The captain didn't warn us to step back.
③ The captain warned us to not step back.
④ The captain ordered us not to step back.
⑤ The captain ordered us don't step back.

10 밑줄 친 우리말을 영어로 바르게 옮긴 것은? |3점|

A Tom can't play the piano well.
B <u>나도 못 해.</u>

① So do I.   ② So can't I.
③ Neither do I.   ④ Neither can I.
⑤ Neither can't I.

최신기출
11 밑줄 친 부분으로 시작하여 문장을 다시 쓸 때, 표시된 위치에 오는 단어는? |4점|

My uncle's house stands <u>on the hill</u>.
→ On the hill ▢ ▢ ▢ ▢ .

① my   ② uncle's   ③ stands
④ house   ⑤ does

12 다음 중 대화가 어법상 틀린 것은? |4점|

① A I am good at dancing.
   B So is Mike. He's a good dancer.
② A Tom doesn't like soccer.
   B Neither do I. I think it's boring.
③ A He can't go camping.
   B Neither can I. I'll be busy.
④ A She passed the vocabulary test.
   B So did James. He studied hard.
⑤ A I'm afraid of spiders.
   B So do I. I don't like hairy legs.

13 밑줄 친 부분의 쓰임이 나머지와 <u>다른</u> 것은? |4점|

① It was a tablet computer <u>that</u> I bought.
② It was two days ago <u>that</u> he came back.
③ It was on the street <u>that</u> he saw me.
④ It was shocking <u>that</u> she failed the test.
⑤ It was the accident <u>that</u> we were talking about.

고난도
14 어법상 옳은 문장을 <u>모두</u> 골라 짝지은 것은? |5점|

ⓐ Paul told me that he will use the stairs.
ⓑ My brother asked me if I could help him.
ⓒ The teacher asked us who had broken the window.
ⓓ She asked James where had he bought the sneakers.

① ⓐ, ⓑ   ② ⓐ, ⓒ   ③ ⓑ, ⓒ
④ ⓑ, ⓓ   ⑤ ⓒ, ⓓ

15 밑줄 친 did의 쓰임이 〈보기〉와 다른 것은? |4점|

> 보기 I did see him with my own eyes.

① The boys did like to play soccer.
② He and I did our homework together.
③ The math teacher did love her students.
④ They did do their best to win the game.
⑤ All the guests did enjoy the food I cooked.

16 빈칸에 공통으로 들어갈 말로 알맞은 것은? |3점|

- She doesn't eat meat, and _____ her father.
- Jenny doesn't have a smartphone, and _____ Mickey.

① so does
② so doesn't
③ neither is
④ neither does
⑤ neither doesn't

고난도

17 밑줄 친 부분이 어법상 틀린 것의 개수는? |5점|

ⓐ There comes he.
ⓑ On the beach sat the couple.
ⓒ Here and there ran the puppies.
ⓓ My parents do care about my worries.
ⓔ He didn't have any money and neither had I.

① 1개 ② 2개 ③ 3개
④ 4개 ⑤ 5개

서술형

최신기출

18 주어진 문장을 지시대로 바꿔 쓰시오. |6점, 각 3점|

> He made pizza yesterday.

(1) pizza를 강조한 문장으로 바꿀 것

→ _____

(2) yesterday를 강조한 문장으로 바꿀 것

→ _____

[19-20] 그림을 보고 각 사람의 말을 간접화법으로 바꿔 쓰시오. |6점, 각 3점|

19

→ Mary asked John _____

_____ his pen.

20

→ Mr. Smith advised her _____

_____ again.

21 밑줄 친 부분을 강조하는 문장으로 바꿔 쓰시오. |3점|

He <u>reached</u> the top of the mountain.

→ _____

_____

[22-23] 다음 문장을 간접화법으로 바꿔 쓰시오. |8점, 각 4점|

22

Eric said to Mary, "I saw you in the bookstore today."

→ Eric told Mary that _____

_____.

23

Tom asked me, "Are you listening to me?"

→ Tom asked me _____

_____.

24 다음 문장을 밑줄 친 말로 시작하는 문장으로 바꿔 쓰시오. |4점, 각 2점|

(1) A drone flew <u>over my head</u>.

→ _____

(2) Many students were <u>in the waiting room</u>.

→ _____

25 다음 질문에 대한 답을 〈보기〉의 문장에서 찾아 It is/was ~ that 강조 구문으로 쓰시오. |6점, 각 3점|

| 보기 | I saw a red car in front of my school yesterday. |

(1) What did you see in front of your school yesterday?

→ _____

_____

(2) Where did you see a red car yesterday?

→ _____

_____

26 다음 문장을 어법에 맞게 고쳐 다시 쓰시오. |3점|

Under my desk my cat sits.

→ Under my desk _____.

27 대화의 밑줄 친 우리말을 각각 영어로 옮기시오. |4점, 각 2점|

A I enjoy watching soccer games.
B (1) <u>나도 그래(경기 보는 것을 즐겨)</u>.
A But I'm not good at playing soccer.
B (2) <u>나도 그래(축구를 잘 하지 못해)</u>.

(1) _____

(2) _____

부록

동사의
불규칙 변화형

• **A-B-B형**

동사원형	과거형	과거분사형(p.p.)	
bring	brought	brought	가져오다
build	built	built	짓다
buy	bought	bought	사다
catch	caught	caught	잡다
feel	felt	felt	느끼다
find	found	found	찾다
hang	hung	hung	걸다
have	had	had	가지다
hear	heard	heard	듣다
hold	held	held	잡다
keep	kept	kept	유지하다
leave	left	left	떠나다
lose	lost	lost	잃어버리다
make	made	made	만들다
meet	met	met	만나다
pay	paid	paid	지불하다
say	said	said	말하다
sell	sold	sold	팔다
send	sent	sent	보내다
sit	sat	sat	앉다
sleep	slept	slept	자다
spend	spent	spent	소비하다
stand	stood	stood	서다
teach	taught	taught	가르치다
tell	told	told	말하다
think	thought	thought	생각하다
understand	understood	understood	이해하다
win	won	won	이기다

• **A-B-A형**

동사원형	과거형	과거분사형(p.p.)	
become	became	become	~이 되다
come	came	come	오다
run	ran	run	달리다

· **A-B-C형**

동사원형	과거형	과거분사형(p.p.)	
be(am/are/is)	was/were	been	~이다, 있다
begin	began	begun	시작하다
break	broke	broken	부수다
choose	chose	chosen	선택하다
do	did	done	하다
draw	drew	drawn	그리다
drink	drank	drunk	마시다
drive	drove	driven	운전하다
eat	ate	eaten	먹다
fall	fell	fallen	떨어지다
fly	flew	flown	날다
forget	forgot	forgotten	잊어버리다
get	got	gotten	얻다
give	gave	given	주다
go	went	gone	가다
grow	grew	grown	자라다
hide	hid	hidden	숨다
know	knew	known	알다
ride	rode	ridden	타다
see	saw	seen	보다
sing	sang	sung	노래하다
speak	spoke	spoken	말하다
steal	stole	stolen	훔치다
swim	swam	swum	수영하다
take	took	taken	가져가다
throw	threw	thrown	던지다
write	wrote	written	쓰다

· **A-A-A형**

동사원형	과거형	과거분사형(p.p.)	
cut	cut	cut	자르다
hit	hit	hit	치다
put	put	put	놓다
read	read [red]	read [red]	읽다
set	set	set	세우다

부록

비교급·최상급

• 규칙 변화 (-er, -est)

원급	비교급	최상급	
big	bigger	biggest	큰
busy	busier	busiest	바쁜
cheap	cheaper	cheapest	싼
easy	easier	easiest	쉬운
early	earlier	earliest	일찍
friendly	friendlier	friendliest	친근한
funny	funnier	funniest	웃긴
great	greater	greatest	위대한
happy	happier	happiest	행복한
hard	harder	hardest	어려운, 열심히
heavy	heavier	heaviest	무거운
hot	hotter	hottest	뜨거운
hungry	hungrier	hungriest	배고픈
kind	kinder	kindest	친절한
large	larger	largest	큰
lazy	lazier	laziest	게으른
lonely	lonelier	loneliest	외로운
nice	nicer	nicest	멋진
noisy	noisier	noisiest	시끄러운
old	older	oldest	나이 든
poor	poorer	poorest	가난한
pretty	prettier	prettiest	예쁜
sad	sadder	saddest	슬픈
scary	scarier	scariest	무서운
short	shorter	shortest	짧은
slow	slower	slowest	느린
tall	taller	tallest	키가 큰
ugly	uglier	ugliest	못생긴
wet	wetter	wettest	젖은
wide	wider	widest	넓은

· 규칙 변화 (more, most)

원급	비교급	최상급	
afraid	more afraid	most afraid	두려운
beautiful	more beautiful	most beautiful	아름다운
boring	more boring	most boring	지루하게 하는
curious	more curious	most curious	궁금한
difficult	more difficult	most difficult	어려운
expensive	more expensive	most expensive	비싼
famous	more famous	most famous	유명한
foolish	more foolish	most foolish	어리석은
helpful	more helpful	most helpful	도움이 되는
important	more important	most important	중요한
interesting	more interesting	most interesting	흥미있는
nervous	more nervous	most nervous	초조한
popular	more popular	most popular	인기 있는
slowly	more slowly	most slowly	느리게
tired	more tired	most tired	피곤한
useful	more useful	most useful	유용한

· 불규칙 변화

원급	비교급	최상급	
good	better	best	좋은
well	better	best	잘
bad	worse	worst	나쁜
ill	worse	worst	아픈
many	more	most	(수가) 많은
much	more	most	(양이) 많은
little	less	least	적은
late	latter	last	(순서가) 늦은
far	further	furthest	먼

문법 개념과 내신을 한번에 끝내다

문장 구조 시각화로
핵심 문법 개념 CLEAR!

시험포인트 및 비교포인트로
헷갈리는 문법 CLEAR!

더 확대된 실전테스트로
학교 시험 대비 CLEAR!

Grammar clear

중학 영문법
클리어.

ANSWERS

Level 3

동아출판

중학 영문법 클리어.

Level 3

ANSWERS

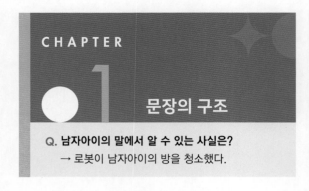

CHAPTER 01 문장의 구조

Q. 남자아이의 말에서 알 수 있는 사실은?
→ 로봇이 남자아이의 방을 청소했다.

UNIT 01 문장의 형식

p. 13

개념 우선 확인 1 주격보어 2 직접목적어
3 목적격보어

A 1 smiled 2 telling 3 calls 4 to play
   5 me
B 1 quiet 2 to 3 for me 4 angry
C 1 cooked us a nice meal
   2 my friends call me Min
   3 to study with Daniel

30초 완성 map

① 동사 ② 주격보어 ③ 목적어
④ 간접목적어, 직접목적어 ⑤ 목적격보어

UNIT 02 목적격보어의 형태 1

p. 15

개념 우선 확인 1 make me sad 2 call me Baby
3 feel the earth shaking

A 1 to play 2 interesting 3 touching
   4 to send 5 their leader
B 1 enter(entering) 2 to exercise
   3 to become
C 1 bark(barking) 2 to use 3 warm
   4 to carry 5 him a liar

30초 완성 map

① 우리의 리더로 ② 행복하게 ③ 가는 것을
④ 노래하는 것을

UNIT 03 목적격보어의 형태 2

pp. 16-17

비교 point 1 carry 2 to carry

개념 우선 확인 1 make them come 2 let me go
3 get my bag stolen

A 1 write 2 install 3 washed 4 frozen
B 1 painted 2 enter 3 change
   4 sung 5 finish 또는 to finish
C 1 let her eat 2 makes me do
   3 has his hair cut
   4 found the window broken

30초 완성 map

① have, clean ② (to) wash ③ repaired

W 서술형 대비 문장 쓰기

p. 18

01 allow me to go out
02 hear the band playing carols
03 helped me finish this work
04 want you to go to the movies
05 me some money 또는 some money to me
06 a big bird fly(flying)
07 me to fix her computer
08 her son paint
09 made me buy
10 heard someone knock(knocking)
11 found his name written
12 told us to wait

시험에 꼭 나오는 출제포인트

p. 19

1 ④
2 ④
3 ② **고득점 POINT** to clean
4 ①, ④ **고득점 POINT** (1) move (2) moved

실전 Test

pp. 20-23

01 ③ 02 ③ 03 ③ 04 ③ 05 ①
06 ② 07 ⑤ 08 ④ 09 ③ 10 ①,④
11 ③ 12 ③ 13 ② 14 ⑤ 15 ②
16 ⑤ 17 ④
18 (1) a text message to my mom
   (2) spaghetti for me
19 made his friends jealous
20 warmly → warm

21 touched → touch(touching)
22 (1) bought me a new bike
    (2) bought a new bike for me
23 advised Jia to get some rest
24 We elected him captain of our team.
25 (1) called (2) call(calling)
26 (1) dance(dancing)
    (2) play(playing) the guitar
27 (1) sweep (2) to wipe (3) clean 또는 to clean

01 「주어＋동사＋수식어구」형태의 1형식 문장이므로 주격보어를 필요로 하는 2형식 동사 become은 들어갈 수 없다.

02 빈칸 다음에 주격보어 역할의 형용사 great가 있으므로 빈칸에는 2형식 동사가 알맞다. see는 1형식, 3형식 또는 5형식 문장에서 쓸 수 있다.

03 4형식 문장을 3형식 문장으로 바꿀 때 make, cook, buy는 간접목적어 앞에 for를, teach와 show는 to를 쓰므로 ⓑ, ⓓ, ⓔ에 for가 들어간다.

04 5형식 문장에서 ask는 목적격보어로 to부정사를 쓴다.

05 make가 사역동사로 쓰였고, 목적어(us)와 목적격보어(stand)가 능동 관계이므로 목적격보어로 동사원형 stand를 써야 한다.

06 have가 사역동사로 쓰였고 목적어(his car)와 목적격보어(repair)가 수동 관계이므로 목적격보어를 과거분사 형태로 써야 한다.

07 전치사 to가 있으므로 주어와 동사 뒤에 「직접목적어＋전치사＋간접목적어」의 어순으로 써서 She lent her umbrella to me.가 된다.

08 get이 '~가 …하게 하다'라는 의미이고 목적어와 목적격보어의 관계가 능동이면 목적격보어로 to부정사를 쓴다.

09 make는 3형식 문장에서는 '~을 만들다', 4형식 문장에서는 '~에게 …을 만들어 주다', 5형식 문장에서는 '~가 …하게 만들다'라는 의미를 나타낸다.

10 help는 목적격보어로 동사원형이나 to부정사를 모두 쓸 수 있다.

11 ③ '나는 이 학생들이 정직하다고 여긴다.'라는 의미의 5형식 문장이므로 목적격보어로 형용사인 honest를 써야 한다.

12 목적격보어로 to부정사(to join)가 쓰였으므로 helped, wanted, told를 동사로 쓸 수 있다. help는 목적격보어로 to부정사와 동사원형을 모두 쓸 수 있다.

13 ① make가 '~을 …으로 만들다'라는 의미의 5형식으로 쓰일 때는 목적격보어로 명사(구)를 쓰므로 전치사 to를 삭제해야 한다. (to a champion → a champion)
③ have가 사역동사로 쓰일 때는 목적격보어로 동사원형을 쓴다. (to wash → wash)

④ leave가 5형식으로 쓰일 때는 목적격보어로 형용사를 쓴다. (to open → open)
⑤ allow는 목적격보어로 to부정사를 쓴다. (read → to read)

14 (A) 「주어＋동사」로 이루어진 1형식 문장이므로 수식어구인 부사 brightly가 알맞다.
(B) 울타리가 칠해지는 수동 관계이므로 목적격보어는 과거분사 형태인 painted가 알맞다.
(C) 지각동사 see는 목적격보어로 동사원형이나 현재분사를 쓰므로 running이 알맞다.

15 주어진 문장과 ②는 5형식 문장이고, ①과 ⑤는 4형식, ③은 1형식, ④는 2형식 문장이다.

16 ① (5형식) ~하게 하다 / (2형식) ~해지다
② (3형식) ~을 가지고 있다 / (5형식) ~하게 하다
③ (2형식) ~한 상태를 유지하다 / (5형식) ~을 …하게 유지하다
④ (4형식) 만들어 주다 / (5형식) ~하게 하다
⑤ (2형식) ~해 보이다

17 ⓑ 수여동사 lend는 3형식으로 쓸 때 간접목적어 앞에 전치사 to를 써야 한다.
ⓓ 사역동사 have의 목적격보어로 동사원형이 와야 하므로 to clean을 clean으로 고쳐야 한다.

18 (1) send는 3형식으로 바꿔 쓸 때 간접목적어 앞에 전치사 to를 쓴다.
(2) make는 3형식으로 바꿔 쓸 때 간접목적어 앞에 전치사 for를 쓴다.

19 「주어＋동사＋목적어(his friends)＋목적격보어(jealous)」의 5형식 문장으로 쓴다.

20 keep은 목적격보어로 형용사를 쓴다. 우리말로 '~하게'라고 해석된다고 해서 부사를 쓰면 안 된다.

21 목적어(someone)와 목적격보어(touch)가 능동 관계이므로 touch를 동사원형이나 현재분사로 써야 한다.

22 수여동사 buy를 3형식으로 쓸 때는 간접목적어 앞에 전치사 for를 쓴다.

23 「advise＋목적어＋목적격보어(to부정사)」 구문을 이용하여 '~에게 …하라고 충고하다'라는 의미의 5형식 문장으로 쓴다.

24 elect는 '~을 …로 선출하다'라는 의미를 나타낼 때 목적격보어로 명사(구)를 쓴다.

25 지각동사 hear의 목적어와 목적격보어가 능동 관계일 때는 목적격보어로 동사원형이나 현재분사를 쓰고, 수동 관계일 때는 과거분사를 쓴다.

26 5형식 문장에서 지각동사 see는 목적어와 목적격보어가 능동 관계일 때 목적격보어로 동사원형이나 현재분사를 쓴다.

27 해석 오늘은 청소하는 날이었다. 우리 선생님은 Tom이 바닥을 쓸게 했다. 그는 수미에게 칠판을 지우라고 했다. 나는 진수가 창문을 청소하는 것을 도왔다. 모두가 교실을

함께 청소했다.
(1) 사역동사 make는 목적격보어로 동사원형을 쓴다.
(2) tell은 목적격보어로 to부정사를 쓴다.
(3) help는 목적격보어로 동사원형이나 to부정사를 쓸 수 있다.

CHAPTER 02 시제

Q. 위 두 문장으로 보아 지금 런던에 있는 사람은?
→ Lisa

UNIT 01 현재완료

p. 27

개념 우선 확인 1 지금도 비가 내리고 있다 2 파리에 가 본 적이 있다 3 지금 시계가 없다

A 1 has lived 2 finished 3 for
　4 been, since 5 have lost
B 1 talked 2 have used 3 Did you live
　4 went 5 didn't leave
C 1 Have you ever seen
　2 has been sick since
　3 have just cooked dinner

30초 완성 map

① has already seen ② have learned
③ 가 본 적이 있다 ④ 가 버렸다

UNIT 02 과거완료, 미래완료, 현재완료진행형

p. 29

개념 우선 확인 1 문을 닫은 후에 내가 도착했다
2 지금도 기다리고 있다

A 1 have been 2 had been
　3 will have lived 4 had already finished
　5 had visited
B 1 had left 2 had already ended

　3 has been working 4 will have been
C 1 have been talking 2 will have repaired
　3 had rained 또는 rained 4 had read 또는 read

30초 완성 map

① had, had, cooked
② will have, will have cooked
③ have, has been, have been cooking

W 서술형 대비 문장 쓰기

p. 30

01 has never tried Thai food
02 had already run away
03 will have finished by
04 have been cleaning the house
05 has just finished
06 has been listening
07 will have lived
08 had already begun
09 I have lived in the same house
10 Have you ever been to
11 I found this bag on the bus
12 They have been waiting for us

시험에 꼭 나오는 출제포인트

p. 31

1 (1) have been (2) has gone
2 ③ **고득점 POINT** did you finish
3 had already left, got
4 has been dancing **고득점 POINT** (1) since (2) for

실전 Test

pp. 32~35

01 ③	02 ④	03 ⑤	04 ④	05 ⑤
06 ③,④	07 ④	08 ③	09 ③	10 ⑤
11 ③	12 ①	13 ⑤	14 ④	15 ⑤
16 ③	17 ④			

18 (1) has been
　(2) will have finished
　(3) had met
19 (1) have been to
　(2) had not had
20 have learning → have been learning 또는
　have learned
21 Have, seen / saw

3 (1) So am I. (2) Neither does my brother.

고득점 POINT (1) did (2) can

4 ⓒ → he

실전 **Test**

pp. 164~167

01 ④	02 ②	03 ④	04 ②	05 ④
06 ②	07 ③	08 ②	09 ④	10 ④
11 ③	12 ⑤	13 ④	14 ③	15 ②
16 ④	17 ②			

18 (1) It was pizza that he made yesterday.
(2) It was yesterday that he made pizza.

19 if(whether) he could lend her

20 not to be late

21 He did reach the top of the mountain.

22 he had seen her in the bookstore that day

23 if(whether) I was listening to him

24 (1) Over my head flew a drone.
(2) In the waiting room were many students.

25 (1) It was a red car that I saw in front of my school yesterday.
(2) It was in front of my school that I saw a red car yesterday.

26 sits my cat

27 (1) So do I. (2) Neither am I.

01 사람인 Peter를 강조하는 「It is/was ~ that(who) ...」 강조 구문이고 보기 중에 who가 없으므로 빈칸에는 that이 알맞다.

02 Many stores are in front of the station.을 부사구로 시작하는 문장으로 바꿔 쓴 것이므로 주어와 동사가 도치된다.

03 that절의 동사는 주절의 시제와 맞춰 will의 과거형인 would가 되고, 인칭대명사 I는 말하는 사람인 he로, you는 듣는 사람인 me로 바꾼다.

04 의문사가 있는 의문문의 간접화법은 「의문사＋주어＋동사」의 어순으로 쓰며, your dream은 my dream으로, is는 주절의 시제에 맞춰 was로 바꾼다.

05 명령문은 간접화법으로 바꿀 때 to부정사로 쓴다.

06 ② 「It is/was ~ that ...」 강조 구문으로 부사구를 강조하여 쓸 때는 부사구 전체를 써야 한다.

07 동사를 강조할 때는 동사 앞에 do동사를 쓰는데, 과거시제일 경우에는 「did＋동사원형」으로 쓴다.

08 ② 주어가 their house이므로 빈칸에는 are가 아닌 is가 들어가야 한다.

09 명령문을 간접화법으로 바꿀 때는 전달되는 문장에 따라 order, advise, warn, ask 등의 전달동사를 쓰고, 부정 명령문은 「not＋to부정사」의 형태로 쓴다.

10 부정문에 대한 동의이므로 「Neither＋동사＋주어」를 쓰고, 동사는 앞 문장의 조동사 can을 쓴다.

11 장소의 부사구로 시작하여 문장을 다시 쓰면 주어와 동사가 도치되어 On the hill stands my uncle's house.가 된다.

12 ⑤ A가 말한 문장의 동사가 am이기 때문에 So am I.라고 답해야 한다.

13 ④는 It이 가주어이고 that절이 진주어인 구문이다. 나머지는 모두 「It was ~ that」 강조 구문이다.

14 ⓐ that절의 시제는 주절의 시제에 따라 써야 한다. (will → would)
ⓓ 의문사가 있는 의문문의 간접화법은 「의문사＋주어＋동사」의 어순으로 쓴다. (had he → he had)

15 〈보기〉와 ①, ③, ④, ⑤의 did는 동사를 강조하기 위해 쓰인 것이고, ②의 did는 '(숙제를) 했다'라는 의미의 일반동사로 쓰였다.

16 두 문장 모두 앞 문장이 doesn't를 사용한 부정문이므로, 이에 대해 '~도 그렇지 않다'라는 의미를 나타내려면 「Neither＋do동사＋주어」를 써야 한다.

17 ⓐ he는 대명사이므로 부사(구)가 앞에 있어도 주어와 동사가 도치되지 않는다.
ⓔ 앞에 나온 문장이 didn't가 쓰인 부정문이므로 had를 did로 고쳐야 한다.

18 「It is/was ~ that」 강조 구문은 강조하려는 말을 that 앞에 쓰고, 문장의 나머지 부분을 that 뒤에 쓴다.

19 의문사가 없는 의문문이므로 접속사 if나 whether를 이용하여 「if(whether)＋주어＋동사」의 어순으로 쓰고, 시제와 인칭대명사를 전달자에 맞춰 바꾼다.

20 명령문을 간접화법으로 바꿀 때는 동사를 to부정사로 쓰며, 부정 명령문은 to 앞에 not을 붙인다.

21 동사를 강조할 때는 do를 동사 앞에 쓰되 시제에 맞게 did로 고치고, 과거시제로 썼던 동사는 동사원형으로 쓴다.

22 주절이 과거인데 큰따옴표 안이 과거이므로 간접화법에서 과거완료로 바꾼다. 인칭대명사나 부사구 역시 전달자와 상황에 맞게 바꾼다.

23 의문사가 없는 의문문이므로 간접화법으로 바꿀 때 「if(whether)＋주어＋동사」의 어순으로 쓰며, 주절의 시제에 맞게 과거시제로 쓴다. 인칭대명사는 전달자에 맞게 바꾼다.

24 장소나 위치를 나타내는 부사구를 문장 맨 앞에 쓰면 「부사(구)＋동사＋주어」의 어순으로 쓴다.

25 「It is/was ~ that」 강조 구문은 강조하려는 말을 that 앞에 쓰고, 문장의 나머지 부분을 that 뒤에 쓴다.

26 장소나 위치를 나타내는 부사구가 문장 맨 앞에 오면 주어와 동사가 도치된다.

27 앞에 나온 내용에 대해 '~도 또한 그렇다/그렇지 않다'라고 말할 때는 「So/Neither＋동사＋주어」 형태로 쓴다. 동사는 앞 문장의 동사를 따른다.

WORKBOOK ANSWERS

UNIT 01 | 문장의 형식
pp. 2~3

A **1** 간접목적어 **2** 주격보어 **3** 수식어구 **4** 수식어구 **5** 직접목적어 **6** 목적격보어
7 목적어 **8** 목적어 **9** 목적격보어 **10** 주격보어

B **1** great **2** look **3** to me **4** going camping **5** me some cookies
6 the baby Ben **7** happy **8** clearly **9** us **10** in the park

C **1** 그 약속을 비밀로 **2** 저에게 5달러를 **3** 피곤해졌다 **4** 그가 정직하다고

D **1** kind **2** very beautifully **3** to the librarian **4** spending time **5** to study law

E **1** goes to school by bus **2** write him a letter **3** bought a new bike for me
4 We found the book useful.

UNIT 02 | 목적격보어의 형태 1
pp. 4~5

A **1** Fluffy **2** his assistant **3** clean **4** to use his computer **5** comfortable
6 calling for help **7** to come home by seven **8** come around the corner
9 to leave a message **10** cleaning his room

B **1** to enjoy **2** open **3** to turn **4** enter **5** asked **6** to cook
7 to exercise **8** looking **9** saw **10** smart

C **1** Cathy를 팀의 주장으로 **2** 내가 콘서트에 가는 것을 **3** 비가 지붕 위에 떨어지는 소리를
4 그녀의 방을 깨끗하게 유지한다 **5** 무언가가 빛나고 있는 것을 보았다 **6** 내가 그녀를 혼자 두기를

D **1** made her very happy **2** saw a deer crossing the road **3** I felt the house shake
4 told me to download the file **5** What makes you so depressed?
6 I watched him building a sandcastle.

UNIT 03 | 목적격보어의 형태 2
pp. 6~7

A **1** 목적어: me 목적격보어: find the bus stop **2** 목적어: us 목적격보어: keep quiet
3 목적어: the door 목적격보어: repaired **4** 목적어: the work 목적격보어: finished
5 목적어: me 목적격보어: know your phone number **6** 목적어: a tooth 목적격보어: pulled out
7 목적어: a dog 목적격보어: hit by a car **8** 목적어: her car 목적격보어: washed
9 목적어: his sister 목적격보어: use his laptop **10** 목적어: me 목적격보어: to find my seat

B **1** recycle **2** played **3** protect **4** to solve **5** make **6** take
7 wrapped **8** helped **9** to bring **10** wake

C **1** 나를 웃게 한다 **2** 내가 물을 많이 마시게 했다 **3** 머리를 잘랐다
4 그가 새 옷을 고르는 것을 **5** 반지를 도난당했습니까

D **1** painted **2** look **3** to accept **4** closed **5** relax 또는 to relax

E **1** He had his computer fixed **2** help my parents to pick apples
3 let me play computer games **4** Flowers will make your room look cozy.

UNIT 01 │ 현재완료

pp. 8~9

A
1 경험　2 계속　3 완료　4 결과　5 완료　6 계속　7 결과　8 경험
9 완료　10 경험

B
1 been　2 has　3 already　4 since　5 began　6 How long
7 never　8 come　9 have not eaten　10 before

C
1 have you been　2 was　3 since she graduated　4 has written
5 have never visited　6 did you meet　7 has gone to　8 have not finished

D
1 He has studied history in London　2 Have you ever met a celebrity
3 I have never been to　4 She has already finished washing
5 How many times have you watched the movie　6 have had a dog since I was ten
7 I have left the book at home　8 We have just heard about the accident.

UNIT 02 │ 과거완료, 미래완료, 현재완료진행형

pp. 10~11

A
1 begun　2 had　3 studying　4 finished　5 have　6 realized
7 had you worked　8 been playing　9 will have seen　10 ended

B
1 had lied　2 had not seen　3 had already met　4 will have lived
5 has been doing 또는 has done

C
1 had just had　2 had helped　3 has been snowing 또는 has snowed
4 will have improved　5 had not left　6 had never been　7 have you been waiting

D
1 will have frozen by tomorrow　2 had had our dog for 10 years
3 had not finished the work yet　4 have you been wearing glasses
5 had been to India once　6 will have arrived home by then
7 have been shopping for three hours　8 She had studied Korean before she came

UNIT 01 | 조동사

pp. 12~13

A 1 능력   2 허락   3 의무   4 능력   5 추측   6 추측   7 허락   8 충고
9 추측   10 의무

B 1 Can   2 should   3 had   4 have   5 can   6 used   7 can't
8 ought not to   9 must not   10 will be able to

C 1 파티에 올지도 모른다   2 일어날 필요가 없었다   3 늦는 게 틀림없다
4 나에게 재미있는 이야기를 해 주시곤 했다   5 사진을 찍으면 안 됩니다

D 1 Can you come 또는 Are you able to come   2 would rather stay
3 don't have to feel   4 used to be   5 had better not give up

E 1 She must be very sad   2 I used to have short hair
3 you must not use your cell phone   4 You had better not touch the paintings.

UNIT 02 | 조동사+have p.p.

pp. 14~15

A 1 should   2 can't   3 must   4 should   5 can't   6 should   7 must   8 may

B 1 must have broken   2 shouldn't have done   3 may have skipped   4 can't have made
5 may not have heard   6 should have listened   7 must have been   8 can't be
9 should not have wasted   10 can't have driven

C 1 비가 왔던 게 틀림없다   2 비밀번호를 잊어버렸을지도 모른다   3 회의에 참석했어야 했다
4 그녀의 제안을 받아들였을 리가 없다   5 싸우지 말았어야 했다

D 1 should have respected   2 must have followed   3 should not have cheated
4 can't have been

E 1 he must have eaten my cookies   2 I should have checked the answers
3 she can't have forgotten my number   4 You should not have stayed up all night.

pp. 16~17

A 1 명사적 용법 2 형용사적 용법 3 명사적 용법 4 명사적 용법 5 형용사적 용법
6 명사적 용법 7 형용사적 용법 8 명사적 용법 9 명사적 용법 10 형용사적 용법

B 1 to eat 2 to rely on 3 how 4 is 5 it 6 to go 7 where to go
8 to sleep in 9 to sell 10 not to be

C 1 수영장에서 입을 수영복이 2 가난한 사람들을 돕는 것은
3 언제 그 프로젝트를 시작할지 4 우리 팀을 이끌 완벽한 사람

D 1 is boring 2 It is good to see 3 not to waste 4 where to plant trees
5 to take care of

E 1 I want to give her this book 2 something important to tell you
3 My goal is to travel all over the world 4 There are many ways to enjoy your holiday.
5 It is not easy to learn foreign languages.

pp. 18~19

A 1 목적 2 감정의 원인 3 결과 4 목적 5 감정의 원인 6 판단의 근거 7 감정의 원인
8 판단의 근거 9 결과 10 목적

B 1 to read 2 to have worked 3 to meet 4 to swim in 5 to be 6 to be moved
7 to travel 8 to have studied

C 1 작가가 되기 위해 2 당신의 파티에 초대되어 3 산을 오르기 위해
4 아흔 살까지 사셨다 5 배가 고팠던 6 그런 실수를 했다니

D 1 grew up to be a famous artist 2 I was excited to go to the rock festival
3 in order to get good grades in math 4 He seems to have had a good time
5 There are some lessons to be learned 6 Her speech was very difficult to understand.

pp. 20~21

A 1 for her 2 for me 3 of you 4 for them 5 for you 6 of Henry
7 for us 8 for students 9 of him 10 for us

B 1 for her 2 for us 3 of him 4 for us 5 kind 6 of you
7 kind enough 8 for our uncle 9 too, to see 10 so busy, couldn't

C 1 네가 경기에서 이기는 것은 2 그녀가 그를 믿다니
3 키가 너무 작아서 그 롤러코스터를 탈 수 없다 4 (그) 위에서 스케이트를 탈 만큼 충분히 단단하게

D 1 so, couldn't go 2 so, can run 3 so, I can't wear them

E 1 wise of her to check the schedule again 2 too complicated for him to solve
3 It is important for us to choose 4 She got up early enough to take the first train.

UNIT 01 | 동명사의 쓰임

pp. 22~23

A **1** 주어 **2** 목적어 **3** 목적어 **4** 보어 **5** 목적어 **6** 주어 **7** 목적어 **8** 보어
9 보어 **10** 주어

B **1** Listening **2** having been **3** collecting **4** is **5** Not wearing
6 buying **7** barking **8** writing **9** finding **10** hearing

C **1** 그 방을 꾸미는 데 많은 시간을 **2** 돈을 저축하지 않았던 것을
3 설거지하는 데 익숙하다 **4** 우리가 그 섬에 가는 것을 막았다

D **1** can't help laughing **2** don't feel like watching **3** Watching baseball games is
4 having won

E **1** Brushing your teeth three times a day **2** is used to cooking for us
3 kept me from sleeping deeply **4** couldn't help staring at the beautiful garden
5 I regret not having taken his advice.

UNIT 02 | 동명사와 to부정사

pp. 24~25

A **1** doing **2** doing, to do **3** to do **4** to do **5** doing, to do **6** doing
7 to do **8** doing **9** to do **10** doing

B **1** barking **2** to run **3** to stay **4** entering **5** turning **6** working
7 to take **8** locking **9** cleaning **10** to turn off

C **1** 나를 깨울 것을 기억해 주세요 **2** 그를 만났던 것을 절대 잊지 않을 것이다
3 그녀의 시간을 낭비하지 않으려고 노력했다 **4** 그 꽃들의 사진을 찍기 위해 멈췄다

D **1** need to repair **2** stop studying **3** remember seeing **4** singing and dancing

E **1** Avoid drinking soda **2** I remember going fishing with my father
3 are trying to help the refugees **4** He promised to take care of my dog

A　**1** when　**2** where　**3** why　**4** where　**5** why　**6** when　**7** how　**8** where

B　**1** when　**2** where　**3** the way　**4** which　**5** why　**6** in which
　　7 why　**8** how　**9** which　**10** the reason

C　**1** 네가 그 문제를 푼 방법을　　**2** 그가 돌아오는 날　　**3** 저 새들이 남쪽으로 날아가는 이유를
　　4 오늘 밤 내가 자게 될 텐트를

D　**1** how you keep healthy　　**2** to know the reason why you love Friday
　　3 Summer is the season when I enjoy surfing.
　　4 LA is the city where the Olympic Games will take place.

E　**1** a garden where I can grow some vegetables
　　2 the reason why I can trust him　　**3** I don't like the way she talks to me.

A　**1** whatever　**2** Whoever　**3** Whatever　**4** whenever　**5** However　**6** whoever
　　7 Whenever　　**8** Wherever

B　**1** Wherever　**2** which　**3** whatever　**4** how　**5** Whoever　**6** Whichever
　　7 whenever　**8** Wherever　**9** whoever　　**10** However cold it is

C　**1** 나는 부산에 갈 때마다　　**2** 누가 전화를 할지라도　　**3** 그가 만지는 것은 무엇이든지
　　4 네가 어디에 가더라도　　**5** 아무리 맛있어 보이더라도　　**6** 네가 어떤 버스를 탈지라도

D　**1** However expensive the car is　　**2** whenever I have trouble studying
　　3 No matter where you go　　**4** The old man wouldn't listen to whatever the others said.
　　5 Whoever wants to be a pianist should practice a lot.

UNIT 01 | 원급·비교급·최상급 비교

pp. 52~53

A **1** high **2** oldest **3** more interesting **4** much **5** more **6** more convenient
7 most beautiful **8** more widely **9** smaller **10** worst

B **1** bigger **2** best **3** as **4** dangerous **5** of **6** going **7** the sweetest
8 more fluently **9** countries **10** much

C **1** 너의 머리카락만큼 길지 않다 **2** 내 파이보다 훨씬 더 크다 **3** 내가 지금껏 본 중에 가장 큰 나무
4 가장 위대한 사람들 중 하나

D **1** in my family **2** the hottest area **3** not as exciting as
4 much(even, far, a lot) better than **5** the busiest cities

E **1** is the most energetic of my friends **2** is much more important than planting them
3 Earth is not as large as Jupiter. **4** She is one of the best students in her class.

UNIT 02 | 여러 가지 비교 구문

pp. 54~55

A **1** tall **2** thinner, thinner **3** more **4** more crowded **5** carefully
6 more expensive **7** much **8** more, healthier **9** often

B **1** thicker **2** as **3** shorter and shorter **4** the more **5** twice **6** more attractive
7 flower **8** more and more exciting **9** as hard **10** tired you get

C **1** 가능한 한 빨리 **2** 점점 더 빨리 움직이기 **3** 오렌지의 두 배만큼 비싸다
4 더 많이 쓸수록, 더 적게 모은다

D **1** is as tall **2** the more curious you become **3** hotter and hotter
4 than any other band

E **1** three times as old as his son **2** No one in my class is more humorous
3 The tree is getting more and more beautiful.
4 The more technology develops, the better our lives become.

CHAPTER 11 | 가정법

UNIT 01 | 가정법 과거, 가정법 과거완료

pp. 56~57

A 1 가정법 과거　2 가정법 과거완료　3 가정법 과거　4 가정법 과거완료　5 가정법 과거
6 가정법 과거완료　7 가정법 과거완료　8 가정법 과거

B 1 were　2 had had　3 knew　4 would have married　5 had been
6 could have bought

C 1 is, can't　2 lied, didn't　3 isn't, can't　4 don't, can't　5 didn't, couldn't

D 1 were　2 wouldn't have come　3 might have bought　4 had invited　5 weren't

E 1 If he had come to the party　2 If she had followed these safety rules
3 I were in your shoes, I would accept his offer

UNIT 02 | I wish, as if, without(but for)

pp. 58~59

A 1 had　2 had come　3 were　4 had met　5 finish　6 have succeeded

B 1 doesn't know　2 didn't tell　3 didn't　4 bought　5 were not

C 1 had　2 would die　3 were　4 hadn't told　5 knew　6 would have arrived

D 1 you had not eaten pizza last night　2 as if she knew everything about pets
3 we would have lost the game　4 I lived in a big city like Seoul
5 the world would be like a desert　6 He talks as if he had won a gold medal.

UNIT 01 | 강조, 도치

pp. 60~61

A
1 the cat   2 at that store   3 come   4 King Sejong   5 love
6 in front of the post office   7 achieve   8 both you and I   9 a small box

B
1 It   2 did call   3 lies a beautiful river   4 does need   5 that   6 he comes
7 that   8 is   9 did   10 Neither

C
1 Around the corner is an antique shop.   2 It was my mistake that made her angry.
3 He did read the book that I bought for him.   4 It was in Busan that my father was born.
5 On the stage appeared the famous actress.

D
1 It was at school that   2 the middle of the park is a tall tree
3 did come to Korea to meet me   4 comes our music teacher
5 can speak two languages, so can I
6 I am not interested in cooking, neither is my sister

UNIT 02 | 화법

pp. 62~63

A
1 that   2 I was   3 if(whether), wanted   4 to come   5 not to run

B
1 that, she, was   2 told, had seen, me   3 if, I was, that   4 why, I, looked
5 told, not to ride

C
1 me to open the window   2 me not to eat at night
3 how I had solved the problem   4 if(whether) she wanted to go to the movies
5 me that he had moved to London three years before
6 told me that she would visit her grandparents the next day

D
1 not to lie to him   2 that he had already seen the movie
3 asked me how long it took to finish the work   4 He told Mia to give him her book.
5 She asked me if I was interested in her painting.

중학 영문법

클리어.

Level 3

ANSWERS

동아출판 영어 교재 가이드

영역	브랜드	초1~2	초3~4	초5~6	중1	중2	중3	고1	고2	고3
문법	[초·중등] 개념서 **그래머 클리어 스타터** **중학 영문법 클리어**		Grammar CLEAR Starter 1	Grammar CLEAR Starter 2	중학 영문법 클리어 1	중학 영문법 클리어 2	중학 영문법 클리어 3			
	[중등] 문법 문제서 **그래머 클라우드 3000제**				그래머 클라우드 3000제 LEVEL 1	그래머 클라우드 3000제 LEVEL 2	그래머 클라우드 3000제 LEVEL 3			
	[중등] 실전 문제서 **빠르게 통하는 영문법** **핵심 1200제**				빠르게 통하는 영문법 1200제 1	빠르게 통하는 영문법 1200제 2	빠르게 통하는 영문법 1200제 3			
	[중등] 서술형 영문법 **서술형에 더 강해지는** **중학 영문법**				서술형에 더 강해지는 중학 영문법 1	서술형에 더 강해지는 중학 영문법 2	서술형에 더 강해지는 중학 영문법 3			
	[고등] 시험 영문법 **시험에 더 강해지는** **고등 영문법**							시험에 더 강해지는 고등영문법		
	[고등] 개념서 **Supreme 고등 영문법**							Supreme 고등영문법		
어법	[고등] 기본서 **Supreme 수능 어법** 기본 실전							Supreme 수능 어법 기본 / Supreme 수능 어법 실전		
쓰기	[중등] 영작 집중 훈련서 **중학 문법+쓰기 클리어**				중학 문법·쓰기 클리어 1	중학 문법·쓰기 클리어 2	중학 문법·쓰기 클리어 3			

문법 개념과 내신을 한번에 끝내다

| 문장 구조 시각화로 | 시험포인트 및 비교포인트로 | 더 확대된 실전테스트로 |
| 핵심 문법 개념 CLEAR! | 헷갈리는 문법 CLEAR! | 학교 시험 대비 CLEAR! |

Grammar clear

중학 영문법

클리어.

WORKBOOK

Level 3

동아출판

중학 영문법 클리어.

Level **3**

WORKBOOK

UNIT 01 문장의 형식

Answers p.26

A 개념 확인

밑줄 친 부분의 문장 성분으로 알맞은 것에 ✔ 표시하시오.

		주격 보어	목적격 보어	목적어	간접 목적어	직접 목적어	수식어구
1	He brought <u>me</u> a cup of coffee.	☐	☐	☐	☐	☐	☐
2	The town looked <u>peaceful</u>.	☐	☐	☐	☐	☐	☐
3	I get up at seven <u>every morning</u>.	☐	☐	☐	☐	☐	☐
4	My aunt lives <u>in Los Angeles</u>.	☐	☐	☐	☐	☐	☐
5	Please give Mr. Gates <u>my message</u>.	☐	☐	☐	☐	☐	☐
6	The book made him <u>a famous writer</u>.	☐	☐	☐	☐	☐	☐
7	I have <u>a sister and two brothers</u>.	☐	☐	☐	☐	☐	☐
8	Where did you put <u>your smartphone</u>?	☐	☐	☐	☐	☐	☐
9	I want you <u>to achieve your dreams</u>.	☐	☐	☐	☐	☐	☐
10	Mr. Jones is <u>my English teacher</u>.	☐	☐	☐	☐	☐	☐

B 어법 선택

괄호 안에서 알맞은 것을 고르시오.

1 His idea sounds (great / greatly) to me.

2 You (look / see) beautiful in that red dress.

3 Jake sent some flowers (for me / to me).

4 Minsu loves (go camping / going camping) on weekends.

5 My grandmother made (some cookies me / me some cookies).

6 They decided to name (the baby Ben / Ben the baby).

7 You made me (happy / happily) when I felt sad.

8 When you speak in front of many people, you should speak (clear / clearly).

9 The teacher asked (us / to us) an important question.

10 I run (the park / in the park) with my dog every morning.

C

해석 완성

밑줄 친 부분에 유의하여 해석을 완성하시오.

1 We should keep <u>the promise a secret</u> forever.

우리는 영원히 _____ 간직해야 한다.

2 Would you lend <u>me five dollars</u>?

_____ 빌려 주시겠어요?

3 She <u>became tired</u> after exercising.

그녀는 운동 후에 _____ .

4 I believe <u>that he is honest</u>.

나는 _____ 믿는다.

D

어법 수정

밑줄 친 부분을 어법에 맞게 고쳐 쓰시오.

1 All the neighbors looked <u>kindly</u>. → _____

2 My sister can sing <u>very beautiful</u>. → _____

3 Harry showed his student card <u>for the librarian</u>. → _____

4 Jane enjoys <u>spend time</u> with her dog. → _____

5 My parents wanted me <u>study law</u> at college. → _____

E

영작

우리말과 일치하도록 괄호 안의 말을 배열하시오.

1 그는 매일 아침 버스를 타고 학교에 간다. (bus, school, to, goes, by)

→ He _____ every morning.

2 나는 일주일에 한 번씩 그에게 편지를 쓴다. (write, a letter, him)

→ I _____ once a week.

3 아버지는 나에게 새 자전거를 사 주셨다. (me, bought, a new bike, for)

→ My father _____ .

4 우리는 그 책이 유용하다는 것을 알게 되었다. (the book, useful, we, found)

→ _____

UNIT 2 목적격보어의 형태 1

Answers p.26

A 개념 확인

각 문장의 목적격보어에 밑줄을 그으시오.

1   I named my cat Fluffy.

2   Mr. Brown made Ted his assistant.

3   We should keep the river clean.

4   Tom allowed me to use his computer.

5   Alice found her new bike comfortable.

6   He heard someone calling for help.

7   My parents told me to come home by seven.

8   I saw the bus come around the corner.

9   We expected him to leave a message.

10   She watched her son cleaning his room.

B 어법 선택

괄호 안에서 알맞은 것을 고르시오.

1   I want you (enjoying / to enjoy) the party.

2   Please leave the window (open / openly) to let in some fresh air.

3   He told me (turn / to turn) off the computer.

4   On my way home, I saw Mina (enter / to enter) the theater.

5   The woman on the train (made / asked) me to move my bag.

6   My mom gets us (cook / to cook) dinner every Sunday.

7   Doctors advise us (exercising / to exercise) at least three times a week.

8   I noticed someone (to look / looking) at me from behind the door.

9   We (had / saw) the girls moving some boxes to the second floor.

10   Ms. Kim considered me (smart / smartly), just because I have a good memory.

밑줄 친 부분에 유의하여 해석을 완성하시오.

1 We elected <u>Cathy the captain of the team.</u>

우리는 _____ 선출했다.

2 My parents allowed <u>me to go to the concert.</u>

우리 부모님은 _____ 허락하셨다.

3 I heard <u>the rain falling on the roof.</u>

나는 _____ 들었다.

4 My sister always <u>keeps her room clean.</u>

내 여동생은 항상 _____.

5 He <u>saw something shining</u> in the dark.

그는 어둠 속에서 _____.

6 She wanted <u>me to leave her alone.</u>

그녀는 _____ 원했다.

우리말과 일치하도록 괄호 안의 말을 배열하시오.

1 그 소식은 그녀를 매우 행복하게 만들었다. (happy, her, made, very)

→ The news _____.

2 나는 사슴 한 마리가 천천히 길을 건너고 있는 것을 보았다. (a deer, the road, crossing, saw)

→ I _____ slowly.

3 나는 어젯밤에 집이 흔들리는 것을 느꼈다. (the house, I, shake, felt)

→ _____ last night.

4 Anna는 나에게 그 파일을 내려받으라고 말했다. (download, me, the file, to, told)

→ Anna _____.

5 무엇이 너를 그렇게 우울하게 만드니? (so, you, what, depressed, makes)

→ _____

6 나는 그가 모래성을 짓고 있는 것을 지켜보았다. (watched, I, a sandcastle, him, building)

→ _____

UNIT 3 목적격보어의 형태 2

Answers p.26

A 개념 확인

각 문장에서 목적어에는 동그라미, 목적격보어에는 밑줄로 표시하시오.

1   The woman helped me find the bus stop.

2   Our teacher made us keep quiet.

3   They had the door repaired.

4   You should get the work finished by noon.

5   Please let me know your phone number.

6   I had a tooth pulled out yesterday.

7   I saw a dog hit by a car.

8   Ms. Wilson had her car washed.

9   He let his sister use his laptop.

10   Could you help me to find my seat?

B 어법 선택

괄호 안에서 알맞은 것을 고르시오.

1   My parents made me (recycle / recycled) bottles and cans.

2   Where did you hear the song (plays / played)?

3   The general had his soldiers (protect / protected) the people.

4   Your teacher will help you (to solve / solving) the problem.

5   How can we (get / make) students focus on their studies?

6   Do your parents let you (take / taken) trips alone?

7   Sally had the box (wrap / wrapped) with red paper.

8   After school, my friends (helped / got) me prepare for the party.

9   Can I get you (to bring / brought) me some cold water?

10   The noise made me (wake / woken) up at midnight.

C
해석 완성

밑줄 친 부분에 유의하여 해석을 완성하시오.

1 His jokes always <u>make me laugh</u>.

그의 농담은 항상 _____.

2 Dr. Robinson <u>had me drink a lot of water</u>.

Robinson 박사님은 _____.

3 He <u>got his hair cut</u> yesterday.

그는 어제 _____.

4 She helped <u>him choose some new clothes</u>.

그녀는 _____ 도와주었다.

5 When did Ms. Smith <u>have her ring stolen</u>?

Smith 씨는 언제 _____ ?

D
어법 수정

밑줄 친 부분을 어법에 맞게 고쳐 쓰시오.

1 My aunt had the roof <u>painting</u> green.　　→ _____

2 His weight loss made him <u>looked</u> older.　　→ _____

3 How can I get them <u>accept</u> my offer?　　→ _____

4 Keep your eyes <u>close</u> for a while.　　→ _____

5 This tea helps you <u>relaxed</u>.　　→ _____

E
영작

우리말과 일치하도록 괄호 안의 말을 배열하시오.

1 그는 어제 컴퓨터를 고쳤다. (fixed, had, he, computer, his)

→ _____ yesterday.

2 매해 가을 나는 부모님이 사과를 따는 것을 도와드린다. (apples, my parents, to, help, pick)

→ I _____ every fall.

3 엄마는 내가 하루에 두 시간 컴퓨터 게임을 하게 해 주셨다. (me, play, let, computer games)

→ Mom _____ two hours a day.

4 꽃은 네 방을 아늑해 보이게 해 줄 것이다. (will, look, flowers, make, your room, cozy)

→ _____

UNIT 1 현재완료

A 개념 확인

밑줄 친 현재완료의 쓰임에 ✔ 표시하시오.

		완료	계속	경험	결과
1	I <u>have been</u> to New York City twice.	☐	☐	☐	☐
2	They <u>have known</u> each other for ten years.	☐	☐	☐	☐
3	She <u>has</u> just <u>finished</u> her breakfast.	☐	☐	☐	☐
4	I <u>have lost</u> my smartphone.	☐	☐	☐	☐
5	<u>Have</u> you already <u>met</u> my brother?	☐	☐	☐	☐
6	He <u>has worked</u> as a farmer since 2010.	☐	☐	☐	☐
7	My uncle <u>has gone</u> to China on business.	☐	☐	☐	☐
8	<u>Have</u> you ever <u>seen</u> a giraffe?	☐	☐	☐	☐
9	I <u>haven't called</u> my dad yet.	☐	☐	☐	☐
10	She <u>has never learned</u> French before.	☐	☐	☐	☐

B 어법 선택

괄호 안에서 알맞은 것을 고르시오.

1 Have you ever (went / been) to Switzerland?

2 Joe (has / have) played the piano for five years.

3 Jimmy has (already / yet) handed in his report.

4 I have volunteered at a dog shelter (for / since) 2015.

5 The concert (began / has begun) 10 minutes ago.

6 (How long / What time) have you been in Paris?

7 I have (ever / never) had Spanish food, but I want to try it.

8 It's getting hotter. Summer has (come / came)!

9 We (have eaten not / have not eaten) anything since this morning.

10 I have watched the film *Frozen* (before / ago).

C
어법 수정

밑줄 친 부분을 어법에 맞게 고쳐 쓰시오.

1 How <u>you have been</u> these days? → _____

2 It <u>has been</u> very hot last summer. → _____

3 She has lived alone <u>for she graduated</u>. → _____

4 He <u>has wrote</u> several novels so far. → _____

5 My grandparents <u>have never visit</u> Japan. → _____

6 When <u>have you met</u> my brother? → _____

7 Simon <u>has been to</u> Paris, so he is not here now. → _____

8 I <u>don't have finished</u> my homework yet. → _____

D
영작

우리말과 일치하도록 괄호 안의 말을 배열하시오.

1 그는 2년 동안 런던에서 역사를 공부했다. (history, he, London, studied, in, has)

→ _____ for two years.

2 너는 전에 유명인을 만나 본 적이 있니? (a celebrity, ever, you, have, met)

→ _____ before?

3 나는 독도에 가 본 적이 없다. (have, I, to, never, been)

→ _____ Dokdo.

4 그녀는 설거지를 이미 끝냈다. (already, she, finished, has, washing)

→ _____ the dishes.

5 너는 지금까지 그 영화를 몇 번 봤니? (watched, the movie, how, you, have, many times)

→ _____ so far?

6 나는 열 살 이후로 개 한 마리를 키우고 있다. (a dog, have, since, had, ten, was, I)

→ I _____ .

7 나는 그 책을 집에 두고 와서 그것을 너에게 보여줄 수 없다. (left, I, have, at home, the book)

→ _____ , so I can't show it to you.

8 우리는 지금 막 그 사고에 관해 들었다. (just, we, the accident, heard, about, have)

→ _____

UNIT 02

과거완료, 미래완료, 현재완료진행형

Answers p.27

A
어법 선택

괄호 안에서 알맞은 것을 고르시오.

1　When I turned on the TV, the game had already (began / begun).

2　They went to bed early because they (have / had) worked all day long.

3　I have been (studied / studying) for the test since last night.

4　The soccer match will have (finish / finished) by 9:30.

5　I (am / have) been writing letters for two hours.

6　We (realize / realized) that our project had failed.

7　Where (have you worked / had you worked) before you started working here?

8　The boys have (being played / been playing) soccer for an hour.

9　If I see this movie again, I (have seen / will have seen) it three times.

10　Mina had already answered all the questions when the test (ends / ended).

B
문장 완성

우리말과 일치하도록 괄호 안의 말을 이용하여 완료 또는 완료진행형 문장을 완성하시오.

1　그녀는 남동생이 자신에게 거짓말했다는 것을 깨달았다. (lie)

→ She found that her brother ＿＿＿＿＿＿＿＿＿＿＿＿＿＿＿＿ to her.

2　그들은 한국으로 이사 오기 전에 눈을 본 적이 없었다. (see, not)

→ They ＿＿＿＿＿＿＿＿＿＿＿＿＿＿＿＿ snow before they moved to Korea.

3　나는 네가 오기 전에 이미 Eric을 만났다. (already, met)

→ I ＿＿＿＿＿＿＿＿＿＿＿＿＿＿＿＿ Eric before you came.

4　우리는 다음 주면 두 달 동안 아프리카에 산 것이 된다. (live)

→ We ＿＿＿＿＿＿＿＿＿＿＿＿＿＿＿＿ in Africa for two months next week.

5　그는 2시 이후로 숙제를 하고 있다. (do)

→ He ＿＿＿＿＿＿＿＿＿＿＿＿＿＿＿＿ his homework since 2 o'clock.

C
어법 수정

밑줄 친 부분을 어법에 맞게 고쳐 쓰시오.

1 When I visited her, she <u>has just had</u> dinner. → _____

2 I wanted to meet the man who <u>has helped</u> me. → _____

3 It <u>has snowing</u> since this morning. → _____

4 I <u>will have improve</u> my English by next year. → _____

5 The train <u>didn't have left</u> yet when I arrived. → _____

6 Ben <u>never had been</u> to the zoo until he was ten. → _____

7 How long <u>are you been waiting</u> here? → _____

D
영작

우리말과 일치하도록 괄호 안의 말을 배열하시오.

1 그 강은 내일이면 얼어 있을 것이다. (have, by, frozen, tomorrow, will)

→ The river _____ .

2 우리는 우리 개가 죽기 전까지 10년 동안 키웠다. (our dog, had, for, 10 years, had)

→ We _____ before he died.

3 내가 Tom에게 전화했을 때 그는 아직 그 일을 끝내지 못했었다. (the work, yet, had, finished, not)

→ When I called Tom, he _____ .

4 너는 얼마나 오랫동안 안경을 써 왔니? (glasses, been, have, you, wearing)

→ How long _____ ?

5 엄마는 나에게 인도에 한 번 가 봤다고 말씀하셨다. (to, India, had, once, been)

→ Mom told me that she _____ .

6 나는 그때까지는 집에 도착해 있을 것이다. (will, then, by, have, home, arrived)

→ I _____ .

7 우리는 세 시간 동안 쇼핑하고 있다. (shopping, for, hours, been, three, have)

→ We _____ .

8 그녀는 한국에 오기 전에 한국어를 공부했었다. (she, before, Korean, had, studied, she, came)

→ _____ to Korea.

UNIT 01 조동사

Answers p.28

A 개념 확인

밑줄 친 조동사의 의미에 ✔ 표시하시오.

		능력	허락	의무	충고	추측
1	My father can play the guitar.	☐	☐	☐	☐	☐
2	May I go home now?	☐	☐	☐	☐	☐
3	You must do your duties.	☐	☐	☐	☐	☐
4	I can fix your computer.	☐	☐	☐	☐	☐
5	It may rain this evening.	☐	☐	☐	☐	☐
6	Jake must be angry with me.	☐	☐	☐	☐	☐
7	Can I buy some chocolate, Mom?	☐	☐	☐	☐	☐
8	You had better take this medicine.	☐	☐	☐	☐	☐
9	The news can't be true.	☐	☐	☐	☐	☐
10	You have to wear a seat belt.	☐	☐	☐	☐	☐

B 어법 선택

괄호 안에서 알맞은 것을 고르시오.

1 (Can / May) you show me your ticket?

2 All of you (should / ought) try your best.

3 You (have / had) better clean up this mess before Mom comes home.

4 You (must / have) to wash your hands before lunch.

5 My brother (can / able to) speak three languages.

6 I (used / was used) to love watching horror movies when I was young.

7 That woman (can / can't) be Ms. Smith. Ms. Smith has returned to her home country.

8 You (ought not to / ought to not) eat a lot of fast food.

9 The baby is sleeping. You (must not / don't have to) speak too loud.

10 He (will can / will be able to) paint his room tomorrow.

C 해석 완성

밑줄 친 부분에 유의하여 해석을 완성하시오.

1 Marie <u>may come to the party</u> tonight.

Marie는 오늘 밤 _____ .

2 He <u>didn't have to get up</u> early.

그는 일찍 _____ .

3 She <u>must be late</u> due to the heavy rain.

그녀는 폭우 때문에 _____ .

4 My grandmother <u>used to tell me interesting stories</u>.

우리 할머니는 _____ .

5 You <u>must not take pictures</u> here.

당신은 여기에서 _____ .

D 어법 수정

밑줄 친 부분을 어법에 맞게 고쳐 쓰시오.

1 <u>Can you able to come</u> to my office at five? → _____

2 I <u>would rather to stay</u> here one more day. → _____

3 You <u>have not to feel</u> sorry for me. → _____

4 There <u>is used to be</u> a library here. → _____

5 You <u>had not better give up</u> in the middle of the race. → _____

E 영작

우리말과 일치하도록 괄호 안의 말을 배열하시오.

1 그녀의 고양이가 아파서 그녀는 틀림없이 무척 슬플 것이다. (be, very, she, must, sad)

→ _____ because her cat is sick.

2 어렸을 때 나는 짧은 머리였다. (short, I, hair, to, used, have)

→ _____ when I was young.

3 운전 중에 너는 네 휴대전화를 사용해서는 안 된다. (use, not, your, must, cell phone, you)

→ While you are driving, _____ .

4 너는 그 그림들을 만지지 않는 게 좋겠다. (the paintings, not, you, better, had, touch)

→ _____

UNIT 02 조동사 + have p.p.

Answers p.28

A 빈칸 완성

〈보기〉에서 알맞은 조동사를 골라 쓰시오.

보기	may	must	can't	should

1 I _____ have called Tom this morning, but I forgot.

2 Mia is very honest. She _____ have lied to me.

3 Someone _____ have taken my umbrella. I can't find it anywhere.

4 I have a stomachache. I _____ not have eaten too much.

5 Mr. Lee _____ have been at the meeting. He was with me at that time.

6 Mike failed the exam. He _____ have studied harder.

7 They _____ have come by taxi. There are no buses after midnight.

8 I think we _____ have met somewhere before. But I'm not sure.

B 어법 선택

괄호 안에서 알맞은 것을 고르시오.

1 My cat (must have broke / must have broken) the vase.

2 You (shouldn't have done / should haven't done) such a foolish thing.

3 Alice (may skip / may have skipped) breakfast. She looks hungry.

4 She (can't has made / can't have made) that terrible mistake.

5 John (may not hear / may not have heard) what I said.

6 You (should have listened / shouldn't have listened) to me, but you didn't.

7 Long time no see! You (must have been / can't have been) busy.

8 My brother has just finished lunch. He (can't be / can't have been) hungry.

9 They (should not waste / should not have wasted) time when they were young.

10 She (must have driven / can't have driven) a car. She doesn't have a license.

밑줄 친 부분에 유의하여 해석을 완성하시오.

1 It <u>must have rained</u> last night.

어젯밤에 _____.

2 My father <u>might have forgotten the password</u>.

우리 아버지는 _____.

3 Peter <u>should have attended the meeting</u>.

Peter는 _____.

4 Michael <u>can't have accepted her offer</u>.

Michael이 _____.

5 You and your brother <u>shouldn't have fought</u>.

너와 네 남동생은 _____.

밑줄 친 부분을 어법에 맞게 고쳐 쓰시오.

1 I <u>have should respected</u> her opinion yesterday.　　→ _____

2 They <u>must had followed</u> his advice last week.　　→ _____

3 You <u>should have not cheated</u> on the last exam.　　→ _____

4 John <u>can't have be</u> there an hour ago.　　→ _____

우리말과 일치하도록 괄호 안의 말을 배열하시오.

1 나는 그가 내 쿠키를 먹은 게 틀림없다고 생각한다. (my cookies, he, eaten, have, must)

→ I think that _____.

2 나는 시험지를 내기 전에 답을 점검했어야 했다. (should, checked, I, the answers, have)

→ _____ before I handed in my test.

3 그녀는 기억력이 좋아서 내 전화번호를 잊었을 리가 없다. (forgotten, have, she, can't, my number)

→ She has a good memory, so _____.

4 너는 밤을 새우지 말았어야 했다. (should, all night, have, you, stayed up, not)

→ _____

UNIT 01 to부정사의 명사적·형용사적 용법

Answers p.29

A 개념 확인

밑줄 친 to부정사의 용법에 ✔ 표시하시오.

		명사적 용법	형용사적 용법
1	She likes to watch movies.	☐	☐
2	My family needs a big house to live in.	☐	☐
3	It is not easy to get a perfect score.	☐	☐
4	My dream is to be a fashion model.	☐	☐
5	This is the best way to make chicken soup.	☐	☐
6	I don't want to download the file.	☐	☐
7	Would you like something to drink?	☐	☐
8	To stay up all night is not desirable.	☐	☐
9	I found it easy to learn English.	☐	☐
10	She has an important decision to make.	☐	☐

B 어법 선택

괄호 안에서 알맞은 것을 고르시오.

1 My little brother hates (eat / to eat) vegetables.

2 Everyone needs someone (to rely / to rely on).

3 I don't know (what / how) to get information on global warming.

4 To make new friends (is / are) hard to me.

5 I found (it / that) difficult to write in a diary every day.

6 It is important (to go / to going) to bed early and get up early.

7 I have not decided (to go where / where to go) during the vacation.

8 You have to bring a tent (to sleep / to sleep in).

9 His goal is (to sell / how to sell) 100 cars this year.

10 Mark promised (to not be / not to be) late for school again.

밑줄 친 부분에 유의하여 해석을 완성하시오.

1 I need <u>a swimsuit to wear in the pool</u>.

나는 _____ 필요하다.

2 It is our duty <u>to help the poor</u>.

_____ 우리의 의무이다.

3 I will let you know <u>when to start the project</u>.

내가 _____ 너에게 알려줄 것이다.

4 She is <u>the perfect person to lead our team</u>.

그녀는 _____ 이다.

밑줄 친 부분을 어법에 맞게 고쳐 쓰시오.

1 To memorize new words <u>are boring</u> for me.　　→ _____

2 <u>This is good to see</u> you here again!　　→ _____

3 He promised <u>to not waste</u> his money.　　→ _____

4 Do you know <u>where plant trees</u>?　　→ _____

5 Ms. Baker has many children <u>to take care</u>.　　→ _____

우리말과 일치하도록 괄호 안의 말을 배열하시오.

1 그녀의 생일에 나는 이 책을 그녀에게 주고 싶다. (to, give, I, this book, her, want)

→ _____ on her birthday.

2 나는 너에게 말할 중요한 것이 있다. (to, something, tell, you, important)

→ I have _____ .

3 나의 목표는 40살이 되기 전에 전 세계를 여행하는 것이다. (goal, all over the world, is, travel, to, my)

→ _____ before I turn 40.

4 너의 휴가를 즐길 수 있는 방법은 많다. (your holiday, there, many ways, are, to, enjoy)

→ _____

5 외국어를 배우는 것은 쉽지 않다. (is, easy, not, to, foreign languages, learn, it)

→ _____

UNIT 02 to부정사의 부사적 용법, to부정사의 시제 · 태

Answers p.29

A 개념 확인

밑줄 친 to부정사의 의미에 ✔ 표시하시오.

		목적	감정의 원인	결과	판단의 근거
1	I went to the market to buy some groceries.	☐	☐	☐	☐
2	He was disappointed to hear the results.	☐	☐	☐	☐
3	Susan opened the box to find it empty.	☐	☐	☐	☐
4	Kate raised her hand to ask a question.	☐	☐	☐	☐
5	I'm very sorry to be late again.	☐	☐	☐	☐
6	She can't be kind to treat her friend in that way.	☐	☐	☐	☐
7	My parents were upset to see the messy house.	☐	☐	☐	☐
8	Sam must be stupid to spend all his money.	☐	☐	☐	☐
9	He left his hometown never to come back.	☐	☐	☐	☐
10	She was standing in line to get a free drink.	☐	☐	☐	☐

B 어법 선택

괄호 안에서 알맞은 것을 고르시오.

1 His book is easy (to read / read to).

2 Mr. Lee seems (to work / to have worked) in China a few years ago.

3 My father was very pleased (to meet / meeting) his cousins.

4 The river is not dangerous (to be swum in / to swim in).

5 Elena grew up (to be / to have been) a jazz pianist.

6 The washing machine needs (to move / to be moved).

7 She wants (to travel / to have traveled) to Europe after she graduates.

8 My mother seems (to study / to have studied) hard in her school days.

C 해석 완성

밑줄 친 부분에 유의하여 해석을 완성하시오.

1 You have to read many books to be a writer.

너는 _____ 책을 많이 읽어야 한다.

2 We were so happy to be invited to your party.

우리는 _____ 정말 기뻤습니다.

3 I got up early to climb a mountain today.

나는 오늘 _____ 일찍 일어났다.

4 My grandmother lived to be 90 years old.

우리 할머니는 _____.

5 He seems to have been hungry at that time.

그는 그때 _____ 것 같다.

6 She must be careless to have made such a mistake.

_____ 그녀는 틀림없이 조심성이 없다.

D 영작

우리말과 일치하도록 괄호 안의 말을 배열하시오.

1 그는 자라서 유명한 예술가가 되었다. (to, grew, be, a, famous, up, artist)

→ He _____.

2 나는 친구들과 록 페스티벌에 가게 되어 신이 났다. (go, excited, to, was, the rock festival, to, I)

→ _____ with my friends.

3 수학에서 좋은 점수를 받으려면 제가 어떻게 해야 하나요? (in, to, in math, get, good grades, order)

→ What should I do _____?

4 그는 지난여름에 즐거운 시간을 보낸 것 같다. (seems, had, he, to, have, a good time)

→ _____ last summer.

5 이 쟁점으로부터 배울 수 있는 몇 가지 교훈이 있다. (to, are, learned, there, some lessons, be)

→ _____ from this issue.

6 그녀의 연설은 이해하기에는 너무 어려웠다. (was, to understand, very, her speech, difficult)

→ _____

UNIT 3 to부정사의 의미상 주어, to부정사 구문

Answers p.29

A 개념 확인

각 문장에서 **to부정사**의 의미상의 주어에 밑줄을 그으시오.

1 It is hard for her to solve this problem.

2 This coffee is too hot for me to drink.

3 It is very kind of you to carry my bags.

4 Jeju-do is the best place for them to live.

5 The desk is too heavy for you to move alone.

6 It was foolish of Henry to give up during the game.

7 His lecture was easy for us to understand.

8 It is not good for students to cheat on exams.

9 It is polite of him to help elderly people.

10 This ladder is long enough for us to pick the apples.

B 어법 선택

괄호 안에서 알맞은 것을 고르시오.

1 It was necessary (for she / for her) to accept his advice.

2 It is exciting (for us / of us) to watch 3D movies.

3 It was very rude (for him / of him) to call me at 2 a.m.

4 Air pollution is a difficult problem (us / for us) to solve.

5 It is (kind / necessary) of you to help children in need.

6 It was careless (for you / of you) to leave the windows open.

7 Mary was (enough kind / kind enough) to take care of my dogs.

8 We are waiting (our uncle / for our uncle) to arrive at the bus station.

9 It was (so / too) dark for me (to see / not to see) her face.

10 I was (too busy / so busy) that I (can't / couldn't) reply to her text message.

밑줄 친 부분에 유의하여 해석을 완성하시오.

1 It was not easy <u>for you to win the game</u>.

_____ 쉽지 않았다.

2 It was foolish <u>of her to believe him</u>.

_____ 어리석었다.

3 You <u>are too short to ride the roller coaster</u>.

너는 _____ .

4 The river was frozen <u>hard enough to skate on</u>.

그 강은 _____ 얼었다.

주어진 문장과 의미가 같도록 빈칸에 알맞은 말을 쓰시오.

1 John was too sick to go to school.

→ John was _____ sick that he _____ _____ to school.

2 She is healthy enough to run a marathon.

→ She is _____ healthy that she _____ _____ a marathon.

3 These sneakers are too tight for me to wear.

→ These sneakers are _____ tight that _____ _____

_____ _____ .

우리말과 일치하도록 괄호 안의 말을 배열하시오.

1 그녀가 일정을 다시 점검한 것은 현명했다. (again, of, to, check, her, the schedule, wise)

→ It was _____ .

2 그 문제는 너무 복잡해서 그가 해결할 수 없었다. (him, solve, too, complicated, to, for)

→ The problem was _____ .

3 우리가 좋은 친구를 선택하는 것은 중요하다. (important, for, it, to, choose, us, is)

→ _____ good friends.

4 그녀는 첫 기차를 탈 만큼 충분히 일찍 일어났다. (got up, the first train, enough, early, she, to, take)

→ _____

UNIT 01 동명사의 쓰임

Answers p.30

A 개념 확인

밑줄 친 동명사의 역할에 ✔ 표시하시오.

		주어	목적어	보어
1	Eating in the theater is not allowed.	☐	☐	☐
2	I enjoy playing the guitar in my free time.	☐	☐	☐
3	My mom is very good at singing.	☐	☐	☐
4	My sister's job is helping people in need.	☐	☐	☐
5	Jane loves mountain climbing.	☐	☐	☐
6	Meeting new people is stressful for me.	☐	☐	☐
7	My sister and I like playing chess.	☐	☐	☐
8	My favorite activity is watching the stars at night.	☐	☐	☐
9	His hobby is taking pictures.	☐	☐	☐
10	Skipping meals is not good for your health.	☐	☐	☐

B 어법 선택

괄호 안에서 알맞은 것을 고르시오.

1 (Listen / Listening) to his music makes me happy.

2 My dad is proud of (being / having been) a soccer player in his school days.

3 Mike is interested in (to collect / collecting) old things.

4 Making good friends (is / are) very important to me.

5 (Wearing not / Not wearing) a suit to the party is acceptable.

6 She spent all her money (to buy / buying) new clothes.

7 The dog's bad habit is (barked / barking) at night.

8 He is thinking of (writing / having written) a novel.

9 They had trouble (to find / finding) their way in the forest.

10 We are looking forward to (hear / hearing) from you soon.

밑줄 친 부분에 유의하여 해석을 완성하시오.

1 She spent a lot of time decorating the room.

그녀는 _____ 썼다.

2 We regret not having saved money for the future.

우리는 미래를 위해 _____ 후회한다.

3 I am used to washing dishes after dinner.

나는 저녁 식사 후에 _____.

4 An oil spill kept us from going to the island.

기름 유출은 _____.

밑줄 친 부분을 어법에 맞게 고쳐 쓰시오.

1 We can't help laugh at his jokes.　　　　　→ _____

2 I don't feel like to watch the horror movie.　　→ _____

3 Watching baseball games are boring to me.　　→ _____

4 He is proud of have winning the prize last year.　→ _____

우리말과 일치하도록 괄호 안의 말을 배열하시오.

1 하루에 세 번 이를 닦는 것은 중요하다. (your teeth, a day, three times, brushing)

→ _____ is important.

2 우리 아빠는 우리를 위해 요리하는 데 익숙하다. (us, used, cooking, to, is, for)

→ My father _____.

3 그 소음은 내가 깊게 자는 것을 막았다. (deeply, me, kept, sleeping, from)

→ The noise _____.

4 우리는 그 아름다운 정원을 응시하지 않을 수 없었다. (garden, help, beautiful, the, staring at, couldn't)

→ We _____.

5 나는 그의 충고를 받아들이지 않았던 것을 후회한다. (his advice, I, not, having, regret, taken)

→ _____

UNIT 02 동명사와 to부정사

Answers p.30

A 개념 확인

빈칸에 알맞은 말에 **모두 ✔ 표시하시오.**

		doing	to do
1	She finished _____ her homework.	☐	☐
2	We continued _____ yoga once a week.	☐	☐
3	Mary wanted _____ the volunteer work.	☐	☐
4	They decided _____ their best.	☐	☐
5	Jerry hates _____ the dishes after meals.	☐	☐
6	My brother and I enjoy _____ crossword puzzles.	☐	☐
7	What are you planning _____ this summer vacation?	☐	☐
8	It is not good to avoid _____ your duties.	☐	☐
9	He managed _____ everything on time.	☐	☐
10	She didn't admit _____ anything wrong.	☐	☐

B 어법 선택

괄호 안에서 알맞은 것을 고르시오.

1 My dog kept (barking / to bark) all night long.

2 He planned (run / to run) his own grocery store.

3 We expect (staying / to stay) at a fancy hotel.

4 She gave up (entering / to enter) the competition.

5 Would you mind (turning / to turn) off the air conditioner?

6 The engine stopped (working / to work) due to overheating. *overheating 과열

7 They refused (taking / to take) part in the Olympics.

8 He remembers (locking / to lock) the door when he left his house.

9 She never puts off (clean / cleaning) her room.

10 Don't forget (turning off / to turn off) the computer when you are not using it.

밑줄 친 부분에 유의하여 해석을 완성하시오.

1   Please remember <u>to wake me up</u> at seven.

7시에 _____.

2   I will never forget <u>meeting him</u> in Seoul.

나는 서울에서 _____.

3   She <u>tried not to waste</u> her time.

그녀는 _____.

4   We <u>stopped to take</u> pictures of the flowers.

우리는 _____.

밑줄 친 부분을 어법에 맞게 고쳐 쓰시오.

1   You <u>need repairing</u> the roof right now.   → _____

2   Don't <u>stop to studying</u> English.   → _____

3   I <u>remember to see</u> you last semester.   → _____

4   She enjoyed <u>singing and to dance</u> at the festival.   → _____

우리말과 일치하도록 괄호 안의 말을 배열하시오.

1   건강을 위해 탄산음료 마시는 것을 피해라. (soda, drinking, avoid)

→ _____ for your health.

2   내가 어렸을 때 나는 아버지와 낚시하러 간 것을 기억한다.

(with, I, going, my father, remember, fishing)

→ _____ when I was young.

3   많은 국가들이 난민들을 돕기 위해 노력하고 있다. (trying, the refugees, help, are, to)

→ Many countries _____.

4   그는 다음 주말에 내 개를 돌봐주기로 약속했다. (promised, he, my dog, to, of, take, care)

→ _____ next weekend.

UNIT 01 현재분사와 과거분사

Answers p.31

A 개념 확인

밑줄 친 분사의 쓰임에 ✔ 표시하시오.

		명사 수식	보어 역할
1	Look at the <u>sleeping</u> baby.	☐	☐
2	He looked <u>tired</u> after his long trip.	☐	☐
3	My mother picked up pieces of <u>broken</u> glass.	☐	☐
4	Do you know that girl <u>looking</u> at us?	☐	☐
5	There are many students <u>studying</u> in the library.	☐	☐
6	They kept me <u>waiting</u> for half an hour.	☐	☐
7	She read a book <u>written</u> in German.	☐	☐
8	He had two teeth <u>pulled</u> out.	☐	☐
9	Everyone was <u>shocked</u> to hear the news.	☐	☐
10	The boy <u>playing</u> the guitar is Joe.	☐	☐

B 어법 선택

괄호 안에서 알맞은 것을 고르시오.

1 We could hear the birds (singing / sung) in the trees.

2 No one wanted to eat the sausage (burning / burned) by fire.

3 My sister was not (satisfying / satisfied) with her grades.

4 The book that I am reading is very (boring / bored).

5 How about getting your car (washing / washed)?

6 The man (smiling / smiled) at us is my English teacher.

7 I found the movie absolutely (thrilling / thrilled).

8 She looked (confusing / confused) when she heard the news.

9 I saw my mother (waving / waved) to me.

10 Your opinion on our new policy was very (interesting / interested).

밑줄 친 부분에 유의하여 해석을 완성하시오.

1 The police caught a man riding in a stolen car.

경찰은 _____ 타고 있는 한 남자를 잡았다.

2 The coach watched the players playing the game.

그 코치는 _____ 지켜보았다.

3 He got injured during the basketball game.

농구 경기 중에 _____ .

4 The sound of flowing water makes me feel calm.

_____ 나를 차분하게 느끼도록 한다.

5 Can you see that building painted yellow?

_____ 보이니?

밑줄 친 부분을 분사를 이용하여 어법에 맞게 고쳐 쓰시오.

1 Do you know the man wear a black coat?　　　→ _____

2 I don't want to make you disappointing.　　　→ _____

3 The match was so excited that I forgot to call you.　→ _____

4 The man makes a speech is our principal.　　→ _____

우리말과 일치하도록 괄호 안의 말을 배열하시오.

1 바다 위로 떠오르는 태양을 봐. (rising, the sun, the sea, over)

→ Look at _____ .

2 그는 나에게 빨간색 종이로 포장된 상자를 주었다. (wrapped, red, in, a box, paper)

→ He gave me _____ .

3 너는 일 년에 한 번 치아를 검사 받아야 한다. (checked, have, you, your teeth, should)

→ _____ once a year.

4 그녀는 영어로 쓰인 편지를 받고 놀랐다.

(surprised, a letter, in English, she, written, was, to receive)

→ _____

UNIT 02 분사구문

Answers p.31

A
개념 확인

밑줄 친 분사구문의 가장 적절한 의미에 ✔ 표시하시오.

		시간	동시동작	이유
1	<u>Finishing breakfast</u>, she left for her office.	☐	☐	☐
2	<u>Drinking some tea</u>, my mom read her book.	☐	☐	☐
3	<u>It being cold</u>, the road is frozen.	☐	☐	☐
4	<u>Before arriving at the hotel</u>, I called my parents.	☐	☐	☐
5	<u>Getting up late</u>, I was late for school.	☐	☐	☐
6	<u>After seeing the police</u>, the thief ran away.	☐	☐	☐
7	<u>Lying on the grass</u>, she listened to music.	☐	☐	☐
8	<u>Being an honest man</u>, he always tells the truth.	☐	☐	☐

B
어법 선택

괄호 안에서 알맞은 것을 고르시오.

1 (Waiting / Waited) for the subway, I heard someone call my name.

2 (Be / Being) very busy, I can't go there to meet my old friends.

3 The rain (stopped / having stopped), we started the game again.

4 (After clean / After cleaning) your room, you can go out.

5 (Having not / Not having) time, I canceled my dental appointment.

6 (Hearing / Heard) the noise outside, I couldn't concentrate on my homework.

7 (Talk / Talking) on the phone, the man ran down the street.

8 (It being / Being) Sunday today, the restaurant isn't open.

9 (Pressing before / Before pressing) the button, insert a coin.

10 (No wanting / Not wanting) to cause trouble, I didn't tell her what happened.

밑줄 친 부분을 분사구문으로 바꿔 쓰시오.

1 When we heard the news, we jumped for joy.

→ _____, we jumped for joy.

2 As it was a nice day, I walked my dog in the park.

→ _____, I walked my dog in the park.

3 Because I was sick, I had to stay home all day.

→ _____, I had to stay home all day.

4 Since I didn't know the answer, I couldn't write anything down.

→ _____, I couldn't write anything down.

5 When I walked on the street, I saw a famous movie star.

→ _____, I saw a famous movie star.

6 While I am standing on my hands, I can sing.

→ _____, I can sing.

7 Where did you live before you came to Korea?

→ Where did you live before _____?

우리말과 일치하도록 괄호 안의 말을 배열하시오.

1 그의 아들이 자고 있어서 그는 조용하게 말했다. (son, sleeping, his)

→ _____, he talked quietly.

2 돈이 충분하지 않아서 나는 그 자전거를 살 수 없었다. (enough, not, money, having)

→ _____, I couldn't buy the bike.

3 무대 위에서 긴장해서 그녀는 대사를 잊어버렸다. (on, being, nervous, the stage)

→ _____, she forgot her lines.

4 나는 책을 읽던 중에 잠이 들었다. (reading, fell, while, a book, asleep)

→ I _____.

5 내 휴대전화를 집에 두고와서 나는 네 이메일을 읽을 수 없었다.

(leaving, your email, cell phone, read, I, at home, my, couldn't)

→ _____

다양한 분사구문

Answers p.31

A 괄호 안에서 알맞은 것을 고르시오.

어법 선택

1 (Seeing / Seen) from space, the Earth looks blue.

2 (Eaten / Having eaten) too much ice cream, I have a stomachache.

3 (Raised / Raising) on an island, he is very good at swimming.

4 (Frankly speaking / Speaking frankly), I didn't keep my promise.

5 Why do people shoot with one eye (closing / closed)?

6 (Having not finished / Not having finished) my assignment, I was very anxious.

7 John is waiting for Alice with his arms (folding / folded).

8 The stage was empty with the lights (turning / turned) off.

9 (Reading / Having read) the book before, he knows the story.

10 (Been / Having been) sick, she missed several days of school.

B 밑줄 친 부분을 분사구문으로 바꿔 쓰시오.

문장 전환

1 <u>Since we had walked for a long time</u>, we felt tired.

→ _____, we felt tired.

2 <u>After I had finished my report</u>, I went to bed.

→ _____, I went to bed.

3 <u>As I had been hit by a car</u>, I was in the hospital for two weeks.

→ _____, I was in the hospital for two weeks.

4 <u>Because she was tired from work</u>, she took a nap.

→ _____, she took a nap.

5 <u>Because he didn't have any food all day</u>, he is hungry now.

→ _____, he is hungry now.

해석 완성

밑줄 친 부분에 유의하여 해석을 완성하시오.

1 <u>Having read the article</u>, I know about the accident.

_____ 나는 그 사고에 관해 알고 있다.

2 <u>Considering the weather</u>, you had better not drive.

_____ 너는 운전하지 않는 게 좋겠다.

3 <u>Speaking of desserts</u>, the macarons at Molly's are fantastic.

_____, Molly's의 마카롱은 환상적이다.

4 He listened to me <u>with his legs crossed</u>.

그는 _____ 내 말을 들었다.

D
어법 수정

밑줄 친 부분을 어법에 맞게 고쳐 쓰시오.

1 <u>Being treating unfairly</u> at work, she was upset.　　→ _____

2 He left the car <u>with its doors unlock</u>.　　→ _____

3 <u>Generally spoken</u>, kids learn languages fast.　　→ _____

4 <u>Studied English</u> for 10 years, he speaks it well.　　→ _____

E
영작

우리말과 일치하도록 괄호 안의 말을 배열하시오.

1 그녀는 고양이를 팔 안에서 자게 둔 채 TV를 보고 있다. (sleeping, her cat, in, with, her arms)

→ She is watching TV _____ .

2 전에 해외에 간 적이 전혀 없어서 나는 지금 아주 들뜬다. (abroad, never, before, been, having)

→ _____ , I'm so excited now.

3 강풍에 망가져서 창문은 수리되어야 한다. (by, broken, the strong wind, been, having)

→ _____ , the window needs to be repaired.

4 엄밀히 말해서 그 화가의 스타일은 사실주의가 아니다.

(realism, the, isn't, painter's style, speaking, strictly)

→ _____

UNIT 01 수동태의 형태

Answers p.32

A 개념 확인

다음 문장이 능동태인지 수동태인지 ✔ 표시하시오.

		능동태	수동태
1	Everyone has to do their duties.	☐	☐
2	The baby is loved by her parents.	☐	☐
3	A letter is being written by Mr. Baker.	☐	☐
4	My grandmother used to tell stories to me.	☐	☐
5	When was the National Museum of Korea built?	☐	☐
6	The deer disappeared into the forest.	☐	☐
7	His book wasn't read by many people.	☐	☐
8	What were you doing when I called?	☐	☐
9	The date of the meeting may be changed.	☐	☐

B 어법 선택

괄호 안에서 알맞은 것을 고르시오.

1 How many languages (are speaking / are spoken) in Switzerland?

2 The festival (will be hold / will be held) this August.

3 Smart devices (are using / are used) almost everywhere nowadays.

4 I (was not hit / was hit not) by the car, but it was close.

5 When she heard the news, she (seemed / was seemed) very angry.

6 What song (is being playing / is being played) on the radio?

7 The road (is had blocked / has been blocked) by the police.

8 When I arrived, the boxes (were be put / were being put) on the truck.

9 The room (should be cleaned / should been cleaned) right away.

10 When we got to the stadium, we found that the concert (had canceled / had been canceled).

다음 문장을 수동태로 바꿔 쓰시오. (단, 「by+행위자」는 생략할 것)

1 He will release his new album next month.

→ _____ next month.

2 They didn't deliver my food on time.

→ _____ on time.

3 They have buried the wooden box in the forest.

→ _____ in the forest.

4 We are repairing the art gallery now.

→ _____ now.

5 We should build many houses for poor people.

→ _____ for poor people.

6 Someone has already eaten the apples on the table.

→ The apples on the table _____ .

우리말과 일치하도록 괄호 안의 말을 배열하시오.

1 비가 오면, 야구 경기는 중지될 것이다. (be, stopped, will, the baseball game)

→ If it rains, _____ .

2 영화가 다운로드되고 있으니 컴퓨터를 끄지 마. (a movie, downloaded, is, being)

→ _____ , so don't turn off the computer.

3 내 출발은 꽤 오랫동안 지연될 수도 있다. (be, my departure, may, delayed)

→ _____ for quite a long time.

4 깨진 유리창이 지금 교체되고 있다. (is, replaced, the, being, window, broken)

→ _____ now.

5 도난당한 그림은 탐정에 의해 발견되었다.

(painting, the detective, found, by, been, the, has, stolen)

→ _____

UNIT 2 4형식·5형식 문장의 수동태

Answers p.32

A
빈칸 완성

빈칸에 전치사가 필요한 경우에는 알맞은 전치사를 쓰고, 필요 없는 경우에는 ✕ 표시하시오.

1 This doll was made _____ me by my grandma.

2 The Nobel Prize was given _____ Marie Curie in 1911.

3 I am being told _____ a funny story by him.

4 A backpack was bought _____ me by my mother.

5 Was my message sent _____ him by my secretary?

6 Yoga has been taught _____ us by Ms. Lee.

7 A special dessert was cooked _____ her by the chef.

8 Have you been shown _____ the new machine?

9 I was given _____ a big present by my dad.

B
어법 선택

괄호 안에서 알맞은 것을 고르시오.

1 He was seen (run / to run) away from the police.

2 I was made (do / to do) the dishes by my mother.

3 Mr. Green was elected (mayor / to mayor) of our city.

4 A scary story was told (me / to me) by my sister.

5 Mike was made (a manager / for a manager) by the boss.

6 She was expected (winning / to win) the gold medal.

7 Helen is considered (honest / honestly) by her friends.

8 The table was made (for / to) Kate by her father.

9 They were allowed (meet / to meet) the president.

10 She was seen (meet / meeting) Tom in the restaurant.

다음 문장을 수동태로 바꿔 쓰시오. (「by+행위자」를 꼭 쓸 것)

1 He will give the winner the trophy.

→ The trophy _____ .

→ The winner _____ .

2 My father cooked us dinner last night.

→ Dinner _____ last night.

3 My sister named the cat Molly.

→ The cat _____ .

4 They saw Mia painting the house.

→ Mia _____ .

5 The teacher made us clean the window.

→ We _____ .

우리말과 일치하도록 괄호 안의 말을 배열하시오.

1 그가 개를 산책시키는 모습이 몇몇 사람들에 의해 목격되었다. (seen, his dog, walk, was, he, to)

→ _____ by several people.

2 어렸을 때 그는 엄마에 의해 '아기'라고 불렸다. (Baby, was, by, called, his mother, he)

→ When he was young, _____ .

3 당신의 티켓이 며칠 안에 당신에게 보내질 것이다. (will, to, be, you, sent, your ticket)

→ _____ in a few days.

4 그는 인공지능(AI)에 관한 강의를 해 달라는 요청을 받았다. (asked, a lecture, he, to, give, was)

→ _____ on AI.

5 우리는 박물관에서 사진을 찍도록 허락받지 못했다. (were, allowed, pictures, take, we, to, not)

→ _____ in the museum.

6 그는 팀의 주장으로 선출되었다. (was, he, team captain, elected)

→ _____

UNIT 3 다양한 수동태

Answers p.32

A 빈칸 완성

빈칸에 알맞은 말을 〈보기〉에서 골라 쓰시오.

보기	at	of	with	in

1 I'm not interested _____ collecting anything.

2 The sky is covered _____ clouds.

3 Our club is made up _____ 12 members.

4 The town was filled _____ people waiting for help.

5 All of us were tired _____ the endless walking.

6 Are you satisfied _____ the reply?

7 I was surprised _____ the bad situation in Congo.

8 The subway was crowded _____ students.

B 어법 선택

괄호 안에서 알맞은 것을 고르시오.

1 How many children were looked after (her / by her)?

2 Our trip (put off / was put off) because my mother was sick.

3 The class is made up (by / of) 20 students.

4 He is pleased (with / at) today's performance.

5 The lights in the room are (turned / turned on) at 6 o'clock.

6 Ann turned off the TV because she was tired (of / to) watching the news.

7 His new book was laughed at (readers / by readers).

8 They are disappointed (by / at) their son's behavior.

9 Mr. Smith is looked up (to / to by) his students.

10 I am not satisfied (with / by) what you have done.

C 문장 전환

다음 문장을 수동태로 바꿔 쓰시오.

1 A truck ran over a squirrel. *squirrel 다람쥐

→ A squirrel _____ a truck.

2 Volunteers look after abandoned animals. *abandoned 버려진

→ Abandoned animals _____ volunteers.

3 Many Europeans looked up to Mother Teresa.

→ Mother Teresa _____ many Europeans.

4 Many young people didn't laugh at his artwork.

→ His artwork _____ many young people.

5 Fred turns the radio off when he goes to bed.

→ The radio _____ by Fred when he goes to bed.

D 어법 수정

밑줄 친 부분을 어법에 맞게 고쳐 쓰시오.

1 Children should be taken care. → _____

2 My mother was very pleased from my present. → _____

3 The director is looked down by the audience. → _____

4 Computers should turned be off when not in use. → _____

5 The team is made up by 10 people. → _____

E 영작

우리말과 일치하도록 괄호 안의 말을 배열하시오.

1 다섯 마리의 염소가 내 보살핌을 받고 있다. (being, me, care, are, by, taken, of)

→ Five goats _____.

2 '햄릿'은 5막으로 구성되어 있다. (of, five, made, acts, is, up)

→ *Hamlet* _____.

3 누구도 외모 때문에 무시를 당해서는 안 된다. (looked, on, nobody, down, be, should)

→ _____ due to their appearance.

UNIT 01 시간·이유·목적의 접속사

Answers p.33

A

개념 확인

밑줄 친 접속사의 의미에 ✔ 표시하시오.

		시간	이유	목적
1	I like listening to music <u>when</u> I take a walk.	☐	☐	☐
2	He went back home <u>because</u> he had forgotten his bag.	☐	☐	☐
3	<u>As</u> she was tired, she couldn't do her homework.	☐	☐	☐
4	<u>While</u> you were sleeping, Henry called twice.	☐	☐	☐
5	Keep the eggs cool <u>so that</u> they won't go bad.	☐	☐	☐
6	You have to turn off the computer <u>until</u> your mom comes home.	☐	☐	☐
7	I run every morning <u>so that</u> I can stay healthy.	☐	☐	☐
8	<u>Since</u> you are under 15, you can't watch that movie.	☐	☐	☐

B

어법 선택

괄호 안에서 알맞은 것을 고르시오.

1 Heat the butter (because / until) it melts.

2 (As soon / As soon as) you come home, wash your hands.

3 We have been staying in the hotel (till / since) we arrived in London.

4 I saved some money (in order to / so that) I could buy a bike.

5 (Because / Because of) I have a bad cold, I'm staying home all day.

6 When you (are not / will not be) busy, I will visit you.

7 She is enjoying popcorn and Coke (since / while) she watches the movie.

8 Before I (hand / will hand) in my report, I will show it to you.

9 I like carrots very much, (while / since) my brother prefers broccoli.

10 John went to bed early (so as to / so that) get up early.

밑줄 친 부분에 유의하여 해석을 완성하시오.

1 <u>Because it was cold outside</u>, I wore my coat.

_____ 나는 외투를 입었다.

2 He waited for me <u>until the class was over</u>.

_____ 그는 나를 기다렸다.

3 <u>Since I want to sleep more</u>, I skip breakfast.

나는 _____ 아침 식사를 거른다.

4 <u>As I felt tired and hungry</u>, I hurried home.

나는 _____ 서둘러 집에 갔다.

5 Don't disturb me <u>while I'm studying</u>.

_____ 나를 방해하지 마시오.

6 He <u>is studying hard so that he can pass the test</u>.

그는 _____ .

우리말과 일치하도록 괄호 안의 말을 배열하시오.

1 내가 샤워하고 있는 동안 그가 나에게 전화했다. (I, taking, while, was, a shower)

→ _____ , he called me.

2 내가 서울에 온 후로 2년이 되었다. (has, came, I, been, since, it, two years)

→ _____ to Seoul.

3 내가 땅에 떨어지지 않도록 줄을 꽉 잡아라. (I, don't, that, the ground, fall down, so, to)

→ Hold the rope tightly _____ .

4 그는 집에 오자마자 냉장고를 열었다. (he, as, the refrigerator, he, home, opened, came, soon)

→ As _____ .

5 많은 비행편이 폭풍 때문에 취소되었다. (many, the storm, canceled, because, flights, were, of)

→ _____

6 날씨가 더 따뜻해지고 있어서 사람들은 여름옷을 사고 싶어한다.

(people, summer clothes, it, warmer, as, is, want, getting, to buy)

→ _____

UNIT 2 조건·양보의 접속사, 명사절을 이끄는 접속사

Answers p.33

A 개념 확인

밑줄 친 접속사의 의미에 ✔ 표시하시오.

		조건	양보	'~인지'
1	<u>Though</u> it is still cold, we will go camping.	☐	☐	☐
2	<u>If</u> you turn to the left, you will see the City Hall.	☐	☐	☐
3	I don't know <u>if</u> she will visit me tomorrow.	☐	☐	☐
4	<u>Although</u> he is 40, he recently entered college.	☐	☐	☐
5	We won't wait for you <u>unless</u> you call us.	☐	☐	☐
6	We will be late <u>if</u> we don't hurry.	☐	☐	☐
7	<u>Even though</u> he knew the answer, he didn't say anything.	☐	☐	☐
8	The question is <u>whether</u> Mia knew the truth.	☐	☐	☐

B 어법 선택

괄호 안에서 알맞은 것을 고르시오.

1   I am not going to the party (if / unless) my sister doesn't go.

2   I wonder (if / though) she will have dinner with us tonight.

3   Unless he (returns / doesn't return) your book, you will have to borrow mine.

4   (Although / If) she is rich, she is not satisfied with what she has.

5   I can't decide if I (go / will go) to London to study English.

6   (Despite / Though) he worked out hard, he failed to lose weight.

7   If you (cheat / will cheat) on exams, you'll be punished.

8   (If / Whether) you will succeed depends on your efforts.

9   You can't play computer games (if / unless) you finish your homework.

10   (Though / Because) I've studied French for five years, I'm not good at speaking it.

C
해석 완성

밑줄 친 부분에 유의하여 해석을 완성하시오.

1 If you know the answer, raise your hand.

_____ 손을 드세요.

2 I got up late even though I went to bed early.

나는 _____ 늦게 일어났다.

3 I will be happy unless she forgets her promise.

_____ 나는 기쁠 것이다.

4 Do you know if she is home?

너는 _____ 아니?

5 Whether he finished the work is not important.

_____ 중요하지 않다.

6 Even though he failed, he won't give up his dream.

_____, 꿈을 포기하지 않을 것이다.

D
영작

우리말과 일치하도록 괄호 안의 말을 배열하시오.

1 네가 충분한 돈을 가지고 있지 않으면 내가 너에게 좀 빌려줄게. (don't, money, have, if, enough, you)

→ _____, I'll lend some to you.

2 우리는 최선을 다했지만 그 경기에서 졌다. (we, best, our, even, tried, though)

→ We lost the game _____.

3 그는 겨우 아홉 살이지만 뛰어난 기타 연주자이다. (he, although, only, is, nine)

→ _____, he is a good guitar player.

4 나는 그녀가 경기에서 이길지 궁금하다. (wonder, win, will, I, she, if, the game)

→ _____

5 그가 오지 않으면 우리는 파티를 연기할 것이다. (will, unless, we, he, put off, comes, the party)

→ _____

UNIT 3 상관접속사, 간접의문문

Answers p.33

A 어법 선택

괄호 안에서 알맞은 것을 고르시오.

1 The detective didn't know (what / whether) he was the thief or not.

2 Both you (and / or) I have to take part in the opening ceremony.

3 Mike speaks (either / neither) Spanish nor Russian.

4 (Do you believe why / Why do you believe) he is not guilty?

5 Your sister, as well as you, (need / needs) to help me clean the house.

6 Her new book is not only interesting but also (humor / humorous).

7 Do you know when you (become / will become) the head chef?

8 I want to know (what you want / what do you want) for your birthday.

9 I wonder (who / if) made these chocolate cookies.

10 You can go to the museum by bus as well as (taking a subway / by subway).

B 문장 전환

두 문장을 간접의문문을 이용하여 한 문장으로 바꿔 쓰시오.

1 I don't know. + Where did I put my cell phone?

→ _____

2 Let me know. + What happened?

→ _____

3 We wonder. + Will you give up?

→ _____

4 Do you think? + What is he planning to do?

→ _____

5 Do you know? + Did he return the book?

→ _____

밑줄 친 부분에 유의하여 해석을 완성하시오.

1 He <u>wanted neither money nor honor</u>.

그는 _____.

2 Mike is good at <u>dancing as well as singing</u>.

Mike는 _____ 잘한다.

3 <u>How</u> do you think <u>he made this robot</u>?

너는 _____ 생각하니?

밑줄 친 부분을 어법에 맞게 고쳐 쓰시오.

1 <u>Both you and I was</u> wrong.   → _____

2 I don't know <u>if has he been</u> to Africa.   → _____

3 Either you or he <u>have</u> to stand in line.   → _____

4 Can I ask you <u>how many books do you have</u>?   → _____

5 He not only saved the children <u>but also curing them</u>. → _____

우리말과 일치하도록 괄호 안의 말을 배열하시오.

1 나는 네가 얼마나 오래 이곳에 머물 것인지 궁금하다. (here, to, you, long, are, stay, how, going)

→ I wonder _____.

2 내 꿈은 디자이너나 건축가가 되는 것이다. (an architect, either, or, a designer, become, to)

→ My dream is _____.

3 나는 그가 오늘 오는지 내일 오는지 모른다. (today, is, whether, or, tomorrow, he, coming)

→ I don't know _____.

4 내 여동생도 나도 어젯밤에 TV를 보지 않았다. (neither, watched, my sister, I, nor, TV)

→ _____ last night.

5 너는 그가 언제 집에 도착할 거라고 생각하니? (home, when, arrive, you, will, think, do, he)

→ _____

UNIT 1 관계대명사의 종류, 관계대명사 what

Answers p.34

A 개념 확인

밑줄 친 관계대명사의 역할에 ✔ 표시하시오.

		주격	목적격	소유격
1	Henry has a bike <u>which</u> is very expensive.	☐	☐	☐
2	This is the book <u>that</u> my friend lent to me.	☐	☐	☐
3	He was the thief <u>who</u> stole my car.	☐	☐	☐
4	I have a friend <u>whose</u> father is a pilot.	☐	☐	☐
5	She is the only person <u>that</u> can solve this problem.	☐	☐	☐
6	The actor <u>who</u> I like the most came to Korea.	☐	☐	☐
7	Look at the house <u>whose</u> roof is green.	☐	☐	☐
8	I have a lot of work <u>which</u> I have to finish today.	☐	☐	☐
9	I saw a mountain <u>whose</u> top was covered with snow.	☐	☐	☐
10	Sue is the girl <u>whom</u> I met at the Christmas party.	☐	☐	☐

B 어법 선택

괄호 안에서 알맞은 것을 고르시오.

1 (That / What) he did was a big mistake.

2 I like people (who / whom) have a sense of humor.

3 Have you seen a book (which / whose) cover is made of leather?

4 Mom bought me the camera (what / that) I wanted.

5 Tears remove harmful matter that (enter / enters) our eyes.

6 You have to appreciate (which / what) you have.

7 The girls that you met in London (is / are) my sisters.

8 That dog (whose / that) tail is very short is mine.

9 I will never forget (that / what) you did for me.

10 She is the one (who / which) built this building.

밑줄 친 부분에 유의하여 해석을 완성하시오.

1 I'm not interested in <u>what you want.</u>

나는 _____에 관심이 없다.

2 <u>That girl whose hair is red</u> is my cousin.

_____ 내 사촌이다.

3 John lives <u>in a house that is 30 years old.</u>

John은 _____ 산다.

4 <u>The woman who I introduced to you</u> is a writer.

_____ 작가이다.

밑줄 친 부분을 어법에 맞게 고쳐 쓰시오.

1 A chef is a person <u>what cooks food</u> in a restaurant. → _____

2 That is exactly <u>which I want to say.</u> → _____

3 The little boy <u>which toy robot is broken</u> is crying. → _____

4 Think about the thing <u>what will make you happy.</u> → _____

우리말과 일치하도록 괄호 안의 말을 배열하시오.

1 아이들은 부모가 하는 것을 따라하는 경향이 있다. (their parents, what, do, copy)

→ Children tend to _____.

2 나는 가난한 사람들을 돕는 것이 목적인 동아리 소속이다. (the poor, whose, is, to help, purpose)

→ I belong to a club _____.

3 나는 긴 휴가를 제공하는 회사에서 일하고 싶다. (that, a company, long vacations, provides)

→ I want to work for _____.

4 우리는 전쟁 동안 손상된 교회를 보았다.

(saw, the war, the church, we, damaged, that, was, during)

→ _____

UNIT 02 주의해야 할 관계대명사의 쓰임

Answers p.34

A 개념 확인

밑줄 친 부분을 생략할 수 있는지 ✔ 표시하시오.

		생략 가능	생략 불가능
1	My uncle has a small shop <u>that</u> is near my house.	☐	☐
2	Here is the message <u>that</u> Mr. Kim sent to you.	☐	☐
3	The boys <u>who are</u> playing soccer are my classmates.	☐	☐
4	There are a few benches <u>which</u> we can sit on.	☐	☐
5	Look at that puppy <u>which is</u> running after a cat.	☐	☐
6	I need some friends with <u>whom</u> I can talk.	☐	☐
7	He was reading a book, <u>which</u> I lent to him.	☐	☐
8	This is a machine <u>which is</u> used for sewing clothes.	☐	☐
9	I bought a chair <u>that is</u> made of wood.	☐	☐
10	We will watch the movie <u>that</u> you talked about.	☐	☐

B 어법 선택

괄호 안에서 알맞은 것을 고르시오.

1 I was late for school again, (which / what) made my teacher angry.

2 Global warming is an issue (which / in which) I have been interested.

3 The cat which (hiding / is hiding) under the chair is so cute.

4 There are a few problems about (which / that) we need to talk.

5 Jake came to the party with Mary, (who / which) surprised me.

6 Is this the key (you are looking for / for you are looking)?

7 Those two girls (singing / who singing) on the stage are my daughters.

8 I visited my favorite museum, (which / that) used to be a church.

9 The man to (who / whom) you were speaking is a famous writer.

10 Anna, (who / that) lives in New York, is my best friend.

밑줄 친 부분에 유의하여 해석을 완성하시오.

1 Bella is the woman I love very much.

Bella는 _____ 여자이다.

2 Do you know that girl looking at us?

너는 _____ 아니?

3 He left the town in which he had lived for a long time.

그는 _____ 떠났다.

4 I went to the concert with a friend, who I met at summer camp.

나는 한 친구와 콘서트에 갔는데, _____ .

5 Mike bought a present for his parents, which he gave them after dinner.

Mike는 그의 부모님을 위해 선물을 샀는데, _____ .

우리말과 일치하도록 괄호 안의 말을 배열하시오. (필요한 경우, 문장부호를 추가할 것)

1 그들이 묵고 있는 호텔은 전망이 좋다. (staying, they, at, which, the hotel, are)

→ _____ has a nice view.

2 그는 새 재킷을 입고 있었는데, 그것은 그에게 잘 어울렸다.

(which, his new jacket, on him, good, looked)

→ He was wearing _____ .

3 그녀가 수영하고 있는 강은 매우 깨끗하다. (swimming, the river, in, she, that, is)

→ _____ is very clean.

4 나는 돌보아야 할 아이들이 몇 명 있다. (children, I, care, of, take, a few, have to, that)

→ I have _____ .

5 나는 경기에서 이겼는데, 그것이 우리 가족을 기쁘게 했다.

(won, made, the game, which, I, happy, my family)

→ _____

UNIT 3 관계부사

Answers p.35

A 빈칸 완성

빈칸에 알맞은 말을 〈보기〉에서 골라 쓰시오.

보기	where	when	why	how

1 Do you know _____ the train will arrive?

2 This is the library _____ I usually read books after school.

3 I want to know the reason _____ he didn't call me.

4 We visited the house _____ Shakespeare was born.

5 She is always kind. That is _____ everyone likes her.

6 March is the month _____ a new semester begins in Korea.

7 I explained _____ I cooked the fish.

8 Seoul is a big city _____ many people live.

B 어법 선택

괄호 안에서 알맞은 것을 고르시오.

1 I remember the day (when / where) I saw you at the party.

2 He wanted to go to the river (which / where) he used to swim with his friends.

3 She showed us (the way / the way how) she carved the pumpkins.

4 The castle (which / where) I visited yesterday was built in the 18th century.

5 Do you know the reason (why / how) he rejected the offer?

6 Don't enter the room (which / in which) the baby is sleeping.

7 She failed the exam. That is (how / why) she is so depressed now.

8 I want to know (what / how) the designer made the dress.

9 Chuseok is the day on (which / when) everyone in my family gets together.

10 I can't understand (the way / the reason) why you gave up your plan.

C
해석 완성

밑줄 친 부분에 유의하여 해석을 완성하시오.

1 My hair is not as long as yours.

내 머리카락은 _____.

2 Your pie is much bigger than mine.

네 파이는 _____.

3 This is the tallest tree that I have ever seen.

이것은 _____ 이다.

4 Gandhi was one of the greatest people in history.

간디는 역사상 _____ 였다.

D
어법 수정

밑줄 친 부분을 어법에 맞게 고쳐 쓰시오.

1 I am the youngest of my family. → _____

2 Daegu is hottest area in Korea. → _____

3 Skiing is as not exciting as surfing. → _____

4 I can play the piano very better than Michael does. → _____

5 Paris is one of the busiest city in the world. → _____

E
영작

우리말과 일치하도록 괄호 안의 말을 배열하시오.

1 그는 내 친구들 중에서 가장 활력이 넘친다. (of, the, is, most, my friends, energetic)

→ He _____.

2 나무를 돌보는 것이 심는 것보다 훨씬 더 중요하다. (much, important, them, is, more, than, planting)

→ Taking care of trees _____.

3 지구는 목성만큼 크지 않다. (large, as, not, as, Jupiter, is, Earth)

→ _____

4 그녀는 반에서 가장 우수한 학생들 중 하나이다. (the, in her class, best, one, she, students, is, of)

→ _____

UNIT 2 여러 가지 비교 구문

Answers p.36

A 빈칸 완성
괄호 안의 말을 알맞은 형태로 빈칸에 쓰시오.

1 This building is twice as _____ as that one. (tall)

2 As he grew older, he became _____ and _____. (thin)

3 Mr. Miller earned three times _____ than I did last year. (much)

4 No place in my town is _____ than the new mall. (crowded)

5 Handle these paintings as _____ as possible. (carefully)

6 This bag is _____ than any other bag in our store. (expensive)

7 No other animal in the zoo eats as _____ as the elephants. (much)

8 The _____ vegetables you eat, the _____ you will become.
(much, healthy)

9 It is important to exercise as _____ as possible. (often)

B 어법 선택
괄호 안에서 알맞은 것을 고르시오.

1 Your book is three times (thick / thicker) than my book.

2 I will reply to you (as / so) soon as possible.

3 The shadows are getting (short and short / shorter and shorter).

4 The older she got, (the more / the most) she resembled her mother.

5 This car is (two / twice) as expensive as mine.

6 No one is (as attractive / more attractive) than Jack.

7 My mother loves roses more than any other (flower / flowers).

8 The game is getting (more and more exciting / more exciting and more exciting).

9 To pass the test, you must study (as hard / harder) as you can.

10 The more you work, the more (you get tired / tired you get).

밑줄 친 부분에 유의하여 해석을 완성하시오.

1 They will join us <u>as soon as they can</u>.

그들은 _____ 우리와 합류할 것이다.

2 The train started to <u>move faster and faster</u>.

그 기차는 _____ 시작했다.

3 Peaches <u>are twice as expensive as oranges</u>.

복숭아는 _____.

4 <u>The more</u> we <u>spend</u>, <u>the less</u> we <u>save</u>.

우리가 _____, 우리는 _____.

밑줄 친 부분을 어법에 맞게 고쳐 쓰시오.

1 No other animal <u>is not as tall</u> as the giraffe. → _____

2 The more you know, <u>the curious you become</u>. → _____

3 The water became <u>more and more hot</u>. → _____

4 The Beatles were more famous <u>than any other bands</u>.→ _____

우리말과 일치하도록 괄호 안의 말을 배열하시오.

1 Dan은 그의 아들의 세 배만큼 나이가 많다. (as, as, three, his son, times, old)

→ Dan is _____.

2 우리 반의 어느 누구도 Tony보다 유머가 있지 않다. (more, is, my class, no, in, one, humorous)

→ _____ than Tony.

3 그 나무는 점점 더 아름다워지고 있다. (the tree, and, more, beautiful, is, getting, more)

→ _____

4 기술이 더 발달할수록, 우리의 삶은 더 좋아진다.
(better, become, the, develops, technology, more, the, our lives)

→ _____

UNIT 01 가정법 과거, 가정법 과거완료

Answers p.37

A 개념 확인

밑줄 친 부분을 참고하여 알맞은 가정법의 종류에 ✔ 표시하시오.

		가정법 과거	가정법 과거완료
1	If you <u>went</u> to bed earlier, you <u>would not be</u> so tired.	☐	☐
2	You <u>could have been</u> on time if you <u>had caught</u> the bus.	☐	☐
3	If a war <u>broke out</u>, many people <u>would be killed</u>.	☐	☐
4	If you <u>had worked</u> harder, you <u>would have passed</u> the exam.	☐	☐
5	If I <u>spoke</u> French, I <u>could work</u> in France.	☐	☐
6	If he <u>had accepted</u> my offer, he <u>would have worked</u> with me.	☐	☐
7	If I <u>had known</u> your email address, I <u>could have written</u> to you.	☐	☐
8	She <u>would get hurt</u> if she <u>fell</u> from the tree.	☐	☐

B 빈칸 완성

우리말과 일치하도록 괄호 안의 말을 알맞은 형태로 바꿔 쓰시오.

1 내가 키가 더 크다면, 그 사과를 딸 수 있을 텐데. (be)

→ If I _____ taller, I could pick the apple.

2 내가 공을 갖고 있었다면, 축구를 할 수 있었을 텐데. (have)

→ I could have played soccer if I _____ a ball.

3 그가 어디에 사는지 안다면, 나는 그를 방문할 텐데. (know)

→ If I _____ where he lived, I would visit him.

4 그를 사랑했다면, 그녀는 그와 결혼했을 텐데. (will, marry)

→ She _____ him if she had loved him.

5 내가 그였다면, 그녀를 용서했을 텐데. (be)

→ If I _____ him, I would have forgiven her.

6 내가 네 생일을 알았다면, 너에게 선물을 사 줄 수 있었을 텐데. (can, buy)

→ I _____ you a present if I had known your birthday.

C 어법 선택

주어진 문장과 의미가 같도록 괄호 안에서 알맞은 것을 고르시오.

1 If it wasn't raining, you could walk your dog.

→ As it (is / isn't) raining, you (can / can't) walk your dog.

2 If she hadn't lied to me before, I would have believed her.

→ As she (lied / didn't lie) to me before, I (don't / didn't) believe her.

3 If he were young, he could travel the world.

→ As he (is / isn't) young, he (can / can't) travel the world.

4 If I had a ticket, I could go to the concert.

→ As I (don't / didn't) have a ticket, I (can't / couldn't) go to the concert.

5 If I had known you were in the hospital, I could have visited you.

→ As I (don't / didn't) know you were in the hospital, I (can't / couldn't) visit you.

D 어법 수정

밑줄 친 부분을 어법에 맞게 고쳐 쓰시오.

1 If I have been you, I would give up smoking. → _____

2 If I had known he was coming, I won't have come. → _____

3 We might buy that house if we had had more money. → _____

4 If you has invited him, he would have been happy. → _____

5 If the weather isn't so bad, we would go on a picnic. → _____

E 영작

우리말과 일치하도록 괄호 안의 말을 배열하시오.

1 그가 파티에 왔다면, 그는 그녀를 만났을 텐데. (had, if, come, the party, to, he)

→ _____, he would have met her.

2 이 안전 수칙을 따랐다면, 그녀는 부상을 입지 않았을 텐데. (followed, safety rules, she, these, had, if)

→ _____, she wouldn't have been injured.

3 내가 네 입장이라면, 나는 그의 제안을 받아들일 텐데.
(accept, were, I, in, I, his offer, would, your shoes)

→ If _____.

UNIT 02

I wish, as if, without(but for)

Answers p.37

A
개념 확인

우리말과 일치하도록 괄호 안에서 알맞은 것을 고르시오.

1 나에게 여동생이 있다면 좋을 텐데.

→ I wish I (have / had) a little sister.

2 네가 어제 내 생일 파티에 왔으면 좋을 텐데.

→ I wish you (come / had come) to my birthday party yesterday.

3 내 남동생은 마치 자신이 어른인 것처럼 행동한다.

→ My little brother acts as if he (is / were) an adult.

4 그는 마치 자신이 그 영화 배우를 만났던 것처럼 말한다.

→ He talks as if he (meet / had met) the movie star.

5 네가 없으면 나는 내 일을 끝내지 못할 것이다.

→ Without you, I couldn't (finish / have finished) my work.

6 너의 조언이 없었다면 우리는 절대 성공하지 못했을 것이다.

→ But for your advice, we could never (succeed / have succeeded).

B
어법 선택

주어진 문장과 의미가 같도록 괄호 안에서 알맞은 것을 고르시오.

1 He talks as if he knew the answer.

→ In fact, he (knows / doesn't know) the answer.

2 I wish I had told the truth.

→ I'm sorry that I (told / didn't tell) the truth.

3 He acts as if he had seen the accident.

→ In fact, he (don't / didn't) see the accident.

4 I wish you hadn't bought that house.

→ I'm sorry that you (bought / had bought) that house.

5 Without the Internet, we couldn't communicate online.

→ If it (were not / had not been) for the Internet, we couldn't communicate online.

우리말과 일치하도록 괄호 안의 말을 알맞은 형태로 바꿔 쓰시오. (필요한 경우, 조동사나 not을 추가할 것)

1 나에게 새 휴대전화가 있다면 좋을 텐데. (have)

→ I wish I _____ a new cell phone.

2 물이 없다면 모든 생물은 죽을 것이다. (die)

→ Without water, all living things _____.

3 그녀는 마치 내가 어린아이인 것처럼 취급한다. (be)

→ She treats me as if I _____ a child.

4 네가 그에게 비밀을 말하지 않았다면 좋을 텐데. (tell)

→ I wish you _____ him the secret.

5 그는 마치 결과를 이미 아는 것처럼 보인다. (know)

→ He looks as if he already _____ the results.

6 교통체증이 없었다면 우리는 더 빨리 도착했을 것이다. (arrive)

→ Without the heavy traffic, we _____ earlier.

D

영작

우리말과 일치하도록 괄호 안의 말을 배열하시오.

1 네가 어젯밤에 피자를 먹지 않았다면 좋을 텐데. (pizza, had, you, not, night, last, eaten)

→ I wish _____.

2 그녀는 마치 반려동물에 관해 무엇이든 아는 것처럼 말한다.
(knew, if, she, pets, everything, as, about)

→ She talks _____.

3 그녀의 도움이 없었다면 우리는 경기에 졌을 것이다. (the game, we, have, would, lost)

→ Without her help, _____.

4 내가 서울 같은 큰 도시에서 살면 좋을 텐데. (like, in, I, a big city, lived, Seoul)

→ I wish _____.

5 사랑이 없다면 세상은 사막 같을 것이다. (would, like, the world, be, a desert)

→ Without love, _____.

6 그는 마치 자신이 금메달을 땄던 것처럼 말한다. (a gold medal, talks, had, if, he, as, won, he)

→ _____

UNIT 1 강조, 도치

Answers p.38

A 개념 확인

문장에서 강조하고 있는 말을 찾아 밑줄을 그으시오.

1 It was the cat that I was looking for.

2 It was at that store that I bought the flowers.

3 He does come to see her every day.

4 It is King Sejong who I respect the most.

5 I do love you with all my heart.

6 It was in front of the post office that I saw her.

7 My sister did achieve what she had dreamed of.

8 It was both you and I that had to apologize to her.

9 It was a small box that he gave me yesterday.

B 어법 선택

괄호 안에서 알맞은 것을 고르시오.

1 (It / That) was Mr. Song that gave me some useful advice.

2 I (do called / did call) you yesterday to check your schedule.

3 To the south of my town (lies a beautiful river / a beautiful river lies).

4 Michael (does need / do needs) your help.

5 It is abandoned dogs (that / which) Mrs. Green takes care of.

6 Mr. Brown is our soccer coach. Here (comes he / he comes).

7 It was the salmon steak and a green salad (that / what) I ordered.

8 Between the hospital and the bank (is / are) a fancy restaurant.

9 A You went to Australia last year.

 B So (does / did) Sam.

10 A I don't like mathematics.

 B (So / Neither) do my friends.

괄호 안의 지시에 맞게 바꿔 쓰시오.

1 An antique shop is around the corner. (around the corner로 시작하여)

→ _____

2 My mistake made her angry. (my mistake를 강조하여)

→ _____

3 He read the book that I bought for him. (read를 강조하여)

→ _____

4 My father was born in Busan. (in Busan을 강조하여)

→ _____

5 The famous actress appeared on the stage. (on the stage로 시작하여)

→ _____

우리말과 일치하도록 괄호 안의 말을 배열하시오.

1 내가 그를 처음 본 것은 바로 학교에서였다. (was, that, at, it, school)

→ _____ I saw him for the first time.

2 그 공원 한가운데에 큰 나무가 하나 있다. (the park, is, the middle, a, tree, of, tall)

→ In _____.

3 그는 나를 만나러 정말 한국에 왔다. (to Korea, to meet, me, come, did)

→ He _____.

4 여기 우리 음악 선생님이 오신다. (our, teacher, comes, music)

→ Here _____.

5 그녀는 두 개의 언어를 할 수 있고, 나도 그렇다. (speak, so, can, two languages, I, can)

→ She _____, and _____.

6 나는 요리하는 것에 관심이 없고, 내 여동생도 그렇다.

(interested, cooking, am, my sister, is, not, neither, in, I)

→ _____, and _____.

UNIT 2 화법

Answers p.38

A
빈칸 완성

직접화법을 간접화법으로 바꿀 때, 빈칸에 알맞은 말을 쓰시오.

1 Susan says, "I'm happy."

→ Susan says _____ she is happy.

2 Ben asked me, "Where are you from?"

→ Ben asked me where _____ _____ from.

3 He asked me, "Do you want something to drink?"

→ He asked me _____ I _____ something to drink.

4 Kevin said to me, "Come to my house by six."

→ Kevin told me _____ _____ to his house by six.

5 Mr. Kim said to me, "Don't run in the classroom."

→ Mr. Kim told me _____ _____ _____ in the classroom.

B
어법 선택

직접화법을 간접화법으로 바꿀 때, 괄호 안에서 알맞은 것을 고르시오.

1 At that time, she said, "I'm tired."

→ At that time, she said (that / if) (I / she) (is / was) tired.

2 He said to me, "I saw you in the park."

→ He (said / told) me that he (saw / had seen) (me / you) in the park.

3 She asked me, "Are you satisfied with this picture?"

→ She asked me (if / that) (I was / you are) satisfied with (this / that) picture.

4 Jack asked me, "Why do you look so sad?"

→ Jack asked me (why / whether) (I / you) (look / looked) so sad.

5 The man said to me, "Don't ride a bike here."

→ The man (said / told) me (to not ride / not to ride) a bike there.

C

문장 전환

직접화법을 간접화법으로 바꿔 쓰시오.

1 He said to me, "Open the window."

→ He told _____ .

2 The doctor said to me, "Don't eat at night."

→ The doctor advised _____ .

3 She asked me, "How did you solve the problem?"

→ She asked me _____ .

4 Peter asked Amy, "Do you want to go to the movies?"

→ Peter asked Amy _____ .

5 Brian said to me, "I moved to London three years ago."

→ Brian told _____ .

6 Susan said to me, " I will visit my grandparents tomorrow."

→ Susan _____ .

D

영작

우리말과 일치하도록 괄호 안의 말을 배열하시오.

1 그는 나에게 그에게 거짓말하지 말라고 경고했다. (to, him, not, lie, to)

→ He warned me _____ .

2 그는 나에게 그 영화를 이미 봤다고 말했다. (had, he, the movie, already, that, seen)

→ He told me _____ .

3 그는 나에게 그 일을 끝내는 데 얼마나 걸리는지 물었다.
(asked, how, the work, finish, it, long, me, to, took)

→ He _____ .

4 그는 Mia에게 그녀의 책을 그에게 달라고 말했다. (her book, told, give, him, to, he, Mia)

→ _____

5 그녀는 나에게 내가 그녀의 그림에 관심이 있는지 물었다.
(was, me, if, in, interested, I, her painting, asked, she)

→ _____

중학 영문법

클리어.

Level 3

WORKBOOK

영역	브랜드	초1~2	초3~4	초5~6	중1	중2	중3	고1	고2	고3
독해	[중등] 기본서 READING CLEAR									
	[고등] 기본서 Supreme 구문독해 / 유형독해									
	[중·고등] 문장독해 공식으로 통하는 문장독해 기본 완성									
듣기	[중등] 듣기모의고사 LISTENING CLEAR 중학영어 듣기모의고사									
	[고등] 듣기모의고사 Supreme 수능 영어 듣기 모의고사 기본 실전									
기출	[중등] 기출예상문제집 특급기출 (중간, 기말) 윤정미, 이병민									
어휘	[초·중·고등] 영단어, 영숙어 뜯어먹는 시리즈									
	[중·고등] 영단어 보카클리어									

영어 실력과 내신 점수를 함께 높이는
중학 영어 클리어 시리즈

문법 영문법 클리어 | **LEVEL 1~3**

최신 개정판

문법 개념과 내신을 한 번에 끝내다!

- 중등에서 꼭 필요한 핵심 문법만 담아 시각적으로 정리
- 시험에 꼭 나오는 출제 포인트부터 서술형 문제까지 내신 완벽 대비

쓰기 문법+쓰기 클리어 | **LEVEL 1~3**

영작과 서술형을 한 번에 끝내다!

- 기초 형태 학습부터 문장 영작까지 단계별로 영작 집중 훈련
- 최신 서술형 유형과 오류 클리닉으로 서술형 실전 준비 완료

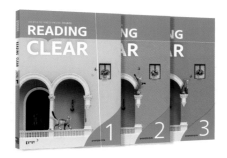

독해 READING CLEAR | **LEVEL 1~3**

문장 해석과 지문 이해를 한 번에 끝내다!

- 핵심 구문 32개로 어려운 문법 구문의 정확한 해석 훈련
- Reading Map으로 글의 핵심 및 구조 파악 훈련

듣기 LISTENING CLEAR | **LEVEL 1~3**

듣기 기본기와 듣기 평가를 한 번에 끝내다!

- 최신 중학 영어듣기능력평가 완벽 반영
- 1.0배속/1.2배속/받아쓰기용 음원 별도 제공으로 학습 편의성 강화